CORNWALL
– A CONCISE ENCYCLOPAEDIA –

MIKE RULE

Cornwall – A Concise Encyclopaedia

© Mike Rule

Cover Design: Tobi Carver

All Photographs: ©Angelicia – (unless otherwise acknowledged)

First Edition published 2011

Published by:
Palores Publications,
11a Penryn Street, Redruth, Kernow TR15 2SP, UK.

Designed & Printed by:
The St Ives Printing & Publishing Company,
High Street, St Ives, Cornwall TR26 1RS, UK.

ISBN 978-1-906845-28-5

CORNWALL
A CONCISE ENCYCLOPAEDIA
An A to Z of most things Cornish

MIKE RULE

Acknowledgements

THE AUTHOR AND PHOTOGRAPHER would like to thank the following for their help: Janet Spargo, Helston Museum, R.N.L.I. Falmouth, Tony Emms, Castle-An-Dinas Quarry, Gerald Penaluna, Oliver Padel, Colin Rescorla, Craftsman of the Silver Ball and the Red Lion Pub, St Columb Major.

Preface

I DO NOT PRETEND to be an expert on anything, let alone an authority on all things Cornish. But what I do have is an insatiable appetite for anything and everything to do with our county. Don't expect a learned treatise on the 150 or so entries within, but read and enjoy them for what they are – little introductions that may lead you down further pathways to more detailed studies or leave you content with that extra little bit of information that will satisfy.

This is not a traditional guidebook in as much as there are many places not included and no attempt has been made to sell a location. In no way is this a slight, but I have to draw the line somewhere. Similarly there are many other famous Cornishmen that might have been included, but a book can only be so big. I am reminded of an observation by a neighbour when contemplating scale. "If it wasn't for scale, a map of Cornwall would be pretty big, wouldn't it?" I know what he meant!

It was difficult to know what to include and even more difficult to decide what to leave out. Don't be upset if your favourite village, town, person or event is missing, or if you find an inaccuracy or opinion with which you disagree. That is your right. I hope you enjoy the contents in the same way that you enjoy all things Cornish.

It would be impossible to offer a bibliography that might guide you to further study, it would be massive! However I must mention one book that has been especially useful and enlightening – Cornish Place-Names by O J Padel, 1988 published by Alison Hodge.

The (q.v.), Latin quod vide, which see, directs you to that subject entry.

Mike Rule,
Threemilestone

About the Compiler

MIKE RULE WAS BORN in Redruth, not the hospital, but at West Trewirgie Road, in the cold winter of late 1946. He was a 'bulge baby', one of a great many born in the year after World War Two when fathers came home from the conflict. Together with his older brother and sister, the family lived in his Uncle Tom's house half way up the hill towards Mount Ambrose. Just as both sets of his grandparents they, like most of the population, lived in rented accommodation. It seemed that at that time you either owned two or three properties, or none at all.

Mike attended East End School, ruled with a rod of iron by the formidable Miss Jose, with music teacher Miss Rowe putting you in the front row, the 'listeners', at Morning Assembly, if like him you were atonal! What would Billy Bray (q.v.) have thought about good Methodists being prevented from praising the Lord! One of the things he did do at school was to study the map of Cornwall on the back cover of the exercise books. It was full of interesting information with centipede-like railway lines all over our land. He used to wonder what it would be like in far off places beyond Bude, and what dangers might exist beyond the mighty Tamar.

Saturday for Mike in the early 50's was a routine of waiting for Father to come home from work at midday. Eating one of Mother's perfect pasties and then going to watch the football – in Redruth rugby was called football – with his brother and father. He had a season ticket. They always sat in section D of the Stand, in fact Mike often still does. Occasionally we would have a 3d raffle ticket for a prize of "30 bob or the ball!" They never did win. Mike can still remember the names of many of the players that would take the field in their proud red jerseys with the full-back wearing number 1, he thinks the hooker was number 9. If the brothers got bored, they could always watch the shunting up at Drump Road or the cows in the field that is now another pitch, and who could ever forget the Winifred Atwell records played before the game?

On the way home they would always call upon their grandparents at Higher Rose Row before continuing on, through Army Barracks, to the other grandparents at East End, passing Sam Lean's pub and that peculiar small of beer and tobacco smoke. Grandad would be listening to the wireless, still then powered by an accumulator, for the football results.

In February 1952 Mike remembers hearing the news on the wireless that King George VI had died and that there was now a new Queen Elizabeth II. On 2nd June 1953 all of Redruth's schoolchildren met at the Recreation Ground to be given a Coronation mug, he's still got it somewhere, a tea-treat bun and a bottle of Jolly's pop. Charlie Delves entertained us with his famous impression of Charlie Chaplin and later we watched show jumping. In 1955 we moved up to the 'big city' of Truro, even the railway station had four platforms! But that is another story.

Mike Rule's love for Cornwall has always been there. He supposes he inherited county-based genes with his grandparents being from Camborne, Redruth, Chynale and Falmouth. Egloshayle and Truro come into the great grandfather mix. One of his great grandfathers from Redruth was a miner in South Africa who returned home only to die a lingering death with phthisis at the age of 46. Another great grandfather was killed by explosives in South Crofty when only in his 20's.

Apart from six years spent living up country, which we Cornish seem to have to endure as part of the process of realising what you are missing when away from home, he has lived in Redruth, Truro, St.Ives, Carbis Bay, Portloe, Gwennap and Threemilestone. A fair cross section in the world of Cornish habitats!

ADAMS, JOHN COUCH
(1819 - 92)

John Couch Adams was the son of a Laneast farmer who as a boy held a fascination with the planets and stars and would spend many a clear night in observation and study. In 1843, at Cambridge University, he became Senior Wrangler, that is he was placed in the first class of the Mathematics Tripos. His fame arose following the mathematical discovery of the planet Neptune in 1845 as a result of a prediction which would explain the anomalies in the observed orbit of Uranus. However, another mathematician, Leverrier, made similar predictions at the same time

AIR AMBULANCE

On the 1st of April 1987 the county saw the first civilian dedicated air ambulance operation take off. Named the First Air Ambulance it was an integral part of the Cornwall Ambulance Service who funded the medical personnel. All of the helicopter costs, a considerable amount of money, were met by donations from the people and businesses of Cornwall. Many gave generously of their time to collect and organise the fund-raising effort. Two names in particular stand out in the early years, Margarette Worden, the first secretary and Bill Pearce who runs the dedicated lottery. Many air-lifted casualties also raised money by various means of sponsorship and covenants.

The first helicopter used was TI (Tango India), a twin-engined MBB Bolko 105. Cruising at 140 mph it could carry two stretchers, uniquely loaded through rear doors. Its compact size made it highly manoeuvrable and able to land almost anywhere. In August 1987 I was fortunate to be air-lifted from a coast-path accident having suffered two broken ankles and one broken leg! It didn't save my life, but it certainly got me to hospital in relative comfort and at a considerable saving in time.

Over the years the helicopters, provided by Bond, have been changed for an improved and more efficient service. Hours of flight have been extended while the service has been copied in many other counties. In December 2010 the 22,000 mission was flown. On average the Air Ambulance attends 1,000 calls each year. As a registered charity the Cornwall Air Ambulance Trust needs to find more than £1.5 million each year! The generous Cornish people are very proud of their red flying ambulance.

The Duchess of Cornwall has become the first official patron of the Cornwall Air Ambulance Trust.

ARCHAEOLOGY

Cornwall is very rich in prehistoric remains. For its size, West Penwith has a greater concentration of these than anywhere in the country, with the possible exception of the Isles of Scilly.

About 4,000 years ago Britain was inhabited by people who came originally from the Mediterranean area. These explorers would have sailed through the Straits of Gibraltar, along the Atlantic coast to Europe. Some settled in what is now Brittany while others reached what is now Cornwall and Scilly. Celts arrived about 2,000 years ago, working the valleys for tin, which they sold to foreign merchants. The English arrived circa 450 A.D. but were never established in the county.

The archaeological remains that are to be seen all around Cornwall, the tools, houses, fortifications and burial places provide the facts and figures of the past. The oldest are the quoits (q.v.) which are stone burial chambers. Standing stones and stone circles date from a similar time.

Good examples are The Merry Maidens and The Nine Maidens near St.Buryan, and The Hurlers near Liskeard. They probably had something to do with burials, but folklore suggests that they were dancers turned to stone for abusing the Sabbath! These quoits and circles were from a time known as The New Stone Age. The people were hunter-gatherers using stone and flint tools. They had no knowledge of metals.

Some 3,500 years ago Britons experimented with bronze, an alloy of tin and copper. Cornwall was an area for bronze manufacture having both the element ingredients available. The Bronze Age people not only made weapons and tools, but also pottery. They lived in stone-walled huts with thatched or turfed roofs. Small scale farming supplemented the hunting and gathering with even a few cattle.

The Iron Age in Cornwall lasted about 400 years from 350 B.C. These Celts built great earthworks or 'castles' on hill or cliff tops. There are many in the county including Chun Castle, Castle an Dinas, Trencrom and Carn Brea. These fortifications were probably only used in times of war rather than lived in permanently. In times of peace Iron Age people lived in villages like that at Chysauster in West Cornwall. (To visit is a must!) This era did not see the start of tin mining, the ore was obtained from the sand and gravel of stream beds. Valuables were stored in underground cave-like structures called fogous. Digs have found smelted tin, pottery, querns, spindle wheels, whetstones, flint and iron tools in these hideaways.

The Romans did come to Cornwall but without an interest to conquer, but probably to trade for tin. A camp was set up at Tregear, near Bodmin, while elsewhere four Roman milestones have been found.

ARMS OF CORNWALL

Historian Ashley Rowe delved deeply into the origins of the county arms and here are some of his findings. The 15 bezants, often incorrectly called 'balls', are often explained in the terms of a ransom or of gold coins affixed to shields. They are in fact a direct link with the days when Cornwall was an independent Earldom. At the time of the Norman invasion, Cadoc, Earl of Cornwall, was believed to have had for his arms a black shield with 15 golden bezants, arranged 5,4,3,2,1. But this was not always so. The earliest authenticated example with bezants is on a shield of Richard Earl of Cornwall, 1209 - 1272, on a carved stone in Westminster Abbey. It shows a lion rampant with a border of bezants, 22 in number! A sword of state now in the British Museum belonged to Edward, Duke of Cornwall, 1470 - 1483, has a Cornish shield with 17

bezants arranged 4,4,4,1,4. This was simply as many as could be fitted in. On Queen Elizabeth's tomb in Westminster Abbey is a shield of 10 bezants 4,3,2,1. It was not until the reign of James I 1566 - 1625, that 15 became normal, but there were still exceptions. In Norden's Survey of Cornwall, 1728, there are 10 on the shield of Albert Edward, Duke of Cornwall.

Cornwall County Council had a shield heraldically described as: Sable fifteen bezants in pile within a Bordure barry wavy of eight Argent and Azure a Chough proper resting the dexter claw upon a ducal coronet Or on the dexter side a fisherman holding over the exterior shoulder a net, and on the sinister side a miner resting the exterior hand on a sledge hammer all proper. The bordure represents the sea and dif-

11

ferences the arms from that of the Duchy. The two men represent Cornwall's primary occupations. The new Cornwall Council seem to have given the two men the chop, but you will see them elsewhere.

Why 15 bezants? Probably because it is a number that nicely fits a shield shape. Bezants are roundels or discs which are always yellow, other colours have different names.

ARSENIC

From the 17th century tin dressing involved burning, or calcining the ore with sand to drive out the sulphur and arsenic. There was little value in the arsenic at this time and the poisonous fumes, instead of being condensed in a flue, were allowed to escape much to the detriment of the local wildlife, especially bees. Of course the effect on the men working the burners was extreme and unquestionably shortened life.

An Arsenic burner

In the mid 19th century the calciner was improved with the use of a labyrinth of pipes up to 1,000 feet long leading to a high chimney stack. Later, in Cornish mining, arsenic had a value with a demand coming from the American cotton fields in their war with the boll weevil.

Much of the arsenic came from the mineral arsenopyrite, known in the county as mispickel. This is a form of fool's gold or mundic where arsenic is in combination with iron sulphide.

ARTHUR, KING

Daphne du Maurier, in her Vanishing Cornwall, 1967, succinctly summarises the 'This is Your Life, King Arthur'. "Here is where Arthur sat or Arthur slept, he feasted upon this stone, he hunted upon these moors. Tintagel was his birthplace, Castle-an-Dinas his hunting lodge, at Slaughter Bridge he received his fatal wound, in the Warbstow Burrows lies his grave." That's about it really. But in Somerset and Wales, and even in Brittany, similar claims are made with equal fervour.

Today we have our heads befuddled with television and Hollywood stories loosely based on Tennyson's Idylls of the King or Malory's Morte d'Arthur, with turreted castles, knights in armour and a magician called Merlin!

Arthur was supposed to have been living in Saxon times, that is in the four to five hundred years before the Norman Conquest. There was a Celtic warrior who may have been Cornish, called Arthur, who fought the Saxon kings, but so little is known of him. He almost certainly wasn't born in Tintagel Castle, where today's obvious remains are of a later Norman origin. The very early ruins may have been monastic, or if military, why choose such an unimportant strategic situation? Similarly nothing of substance is known of King Mark of Cornwall who was supposed to have lived in or about the 6th century. Once again the romantics bring us his nephew Tristan and the Irish Iseult. Modern day Arthurians look for place-name ties, like Camelford must be Camelot. But the name is simply the ford across the River Camel, probably from 'camm' crooked in Cornish, and maybe All as in the River Allen. However there was a Cornish defeat in battle with the Saxons at Slaughter Bridge.

So of King Arthur make what you will. By all means believe that his spirit is in the chough (q.v.) (why did he desert us for fifty years?) and that Excaliber is at the bottom of Dozmary Pool, and when you visit Tintagel be sure to leave your vehicle in Merlin's Car Park and dine at Lancelot's Cafe!

Tintagel Castle

B

BICKFORD, WILLIAM

William Bickford of Tuckingmill invented and patented (1830) the miner's safety fuse for blasting rock. Up to this time numerous fatal accidents occurred with the crude method of firing using goose quills or reeds filled with gunpowder. It was said that Bickford's idea of a safety fuse came to him while watching a rope-maker spinning out his yarn. He introduced a trickle of gunpowder into the centre of the rope as it was spun. After, the rope would be bound with tape and finally varnished to keep out the damp.

In the first year Bickford's factory at Tuckingmill, between Camborne and Redruth, made over 45 miles of fuse and by 1933 was producing 200 miles per day! Factories were to be set up in many parts of the world producing huge quantities of the life-saving safety fuse.

BLIGH, ADMIRAL

A native of St Tudy, he was with Captain Cook in 1772 on the *Resolution* where he obtained the nickname 'Breadfruit Bligh' from the fruit's discovery on that voyage. Well remembered from Hollywood's portrayal of him as a cruel and overbearing character in command of *The Bounty*, leading to the famous mutiny, he was to prove an excellent navigator. He and members of the non-mutinous crew voyaged thousands of miles to safety in an open boat. Bligh made two other voyages to the South Seas and was with Nelson at Copenhagen. That he was certainly not an easy man is shown by his very short stay as Governor of New South Wales.

BODMIN

One of the few Cornish towns not associated with the sea or a river, Bodmin was very important historically. It had religious foundations with a Benedictine Priory here in the mid 6th century, nothing major of which remains. Today's Church of St Petroc (Petrock) is mainly 15th century with later alterations. It is Cornwall's largest church. When St Petroc died, the high prices fetched by authentic relics caused his bones to be raised and transported to Brittany. They were later retrieved in 1177. In the churchyard is the ruin of a chapel of St Thomas Becket, licensed in 1377.

Within the Church are the regimental colours of the Duke of Cornwall's Light Infantry with much military memorabilia. In fact the North Choir is called The Soldiers' Chancel.

During the Cornish Rebellion of 1549 (q.v.) the Mayor was hanged on his own gallows after a jovial dinner!

Once the County Town and having the County Assizes, Bodmin has lost out to Truro. One factor that did the town no good at all was the refusal of local landowners to allow the mainline railway to come through. As a consequence Bodmin was served by branch lines only, almost leaving it a 'backwater' town.

Bodmin Gaol would seem to have been more enlightened than the notorious 'Lanson Gaol'. It is reported that in 1799 that the male prisoners were given tasks such as gardening and stone polishing. The females were given spinning and weaving. All making some small income from their labours.

In the Courts no distinction was made between the seriousness of the crimes the prisoners had committed with respect to their punishment. An example of barbaric indifference is described by historian Charles Henderson, "In 1827 Mary Bennetts, the wife of a respectable farmer, was sentenced to seven years transportation for shoplifting. Her affluence and the trifling value of the stolen articles clearly indicated kleptomania, a condition aggravated by her advanced pregnancy. Without compassion the sentence was carried out."

For many years Bodmin had the mental hospital of St Lawrence caring for over a thousand patients from all over the county. This lunatic asylum, as it was known, gave the Cornish the expression, "She ought be up Bodmin" when referring to someone of mental instability.

Over the years Bodmin has received some bad press. What it needs is a good agent. But I can't recommend Arthur Norway who in 1897 wrote Highways and Byways in Devon and Cornwall, "And of Bodmin, what shall I say? Why if this book was intended to contain a sympathetic description of that struggling hilly town, it should have been entrusted to a Bodmin man, for I know no one else who would be likely to succeed."

A common expression in Cornwall was, "Into Bodmin and out of the World!" The town has considerably increased in size and standing over the recent years. A visit to the gem of the Bodmin and Wenford Railway is a must.

BODMIN MOOR

Cornwall's barren, granite, misty moor that most of us know from the car window as we travel the A30 was originally called Foy Moor. It became changed to the present Bodmin Moor by English map-makers. Its four parishes of Cardinham, Warleggan, St Neot and St Cleer are rich in archaeological remains and fascinating geological formations like The Cheesewring. Cardinham Church has 15th century bench ends and outside one of the best Cornish Celtic crosses of a wheel design.

Warleggan had a most eccentric vicar, the Reverend Densham, there in the 1920's. His odd behaviour and his unapproachableness discouraged many from attending church. Densham responded by setting up cardboard cut-out 'parishoners' to preach to. He caused further upsets by making the Vicarage a fortress surrounded by barbed wire and guarded by dogs. The parishioners being unable to take any more, petitioned the Bishop. Finding no default of Ecclesiastical Law nothing could be done to remove him despite having now an empty church, save the cut-outs. Some years later his body was found in the now empty and lonely vicarage.

The desolate and bleak Dozmary Pool is a place of legend. It is of course not bottomless and a small tree thrown into it did not reappear at Fowey! But Tregeagle (q.v.) may have been there once. Not far away is Bolventor. Not a Cornish name, but a 'bold venture' c1850 with an attempt to set up a farm on the Moor. It is now best known for The Jamaica Inn. Immortalised by Daphne du Maurier's novel about smuggling, it was a staging post inn welcoming travellers on the wild moorland road. The inn's history

according to Henry Douch in his Old Cornish Inns, 1966, goes back at least 220 years and has two possible reasons for its unusual name. It could have reflected the inn's healthy trade in rum, but I prefer the second idea that "someone thought its atmosphere and situation so unlike Jamaica that he thought it worth the cynical comment."

The southern face of the Moor, around St Neot, shows a softer wooded side compared with the rough magnificence of Brown Willy (q.v.) and Roughtor.

In recent years sightings of big cats have been reported in and around Bodmin Moor. With the national press getting hold of the stories, much has been made of the 'Beast of Bodmin'. It would seem very likely that with the increase in exotic pets some would have escaped or been released to fend for themselves. My bet is that they are panthers and pumas!

BOSCASTLE

There are just a few earthworks left of Boterel's Castle which gives this unusual village its name. The narrow S-shaped entrance from the Atlantic looks difficult enough in good weather, but I wouldn't like to attempt it in a gale!

The village is a little way up the Valency Valley, seemingly forever in the shade. Indeed Boscastle has the 'Marmite' factor about it, you either love it or find it unappealing.

Folliott-Stokes in his Cornish Coast and Moors, 1928, falls into the former category. "It is a struggling, picturesque place – a delightful medley of trees, cottages, fragments of streets and orchards, where the cawing of rooks and the song of thrush and blackbird mingle harmoniously with the voices of children and the rhythmic clanging of the blacksmith's forge."

But Mais, The Cornish Riviera, 1923, has a different take, "It is not at all the kind of port to have to make in a storm, and looks as if the natives had gone on putting jetty after jetty on either side in the vain effort to calm a troubled sea…. There are houses on either side of the Valency River, but they are too shut in to attract visitors. It is the sort of place that fine weather does not suit. Its grimness calls for the wild storm that J M W Turner associated with it in his remarkably imaginative picture. I cannot imagine anyone going to Cornwall and making it his headquarters. Its austerity is frightening. It makes no bid to please. It is just a place of extraordinary interest which sometimes one is glad to leave."

Harsh words indeed, but this was written nearly ninety years ago. But not however as harsh as nature would be on 16th August 2004. A flash flood caused extensive damage, witnessed by all on the television news. Residents and visitors were trapped in the houses and cars were swept away to the sea. Sea King helicopters helped in the rescue of 91 people. Miraculously there were no fatalities.

BOSCAWEN, ADMIRAL
The Boscawen family (Lord Falmouth) has its home at Tregothnan overlooking the River Fal. Please note, Boscawen is pronounced Bos CAW en, as in the sound of a crow. Not Bos Cow en as in cattle. Local radio please note!

Edward Boscawen was born in 1711. Later nicknamed 'Old Dreadnought' he saw service in many parts of the world. He fought the Spanish at Porto Bello and Carthagena where he gained credit. His greatest action was the capture of Louisbourg in 1758 which directly led to Wolfe's victory at Quebec and the conquest of Canada. He later represented Truro as an M.P.

BRAY, BILLY
1794 - 1868
Billy Bray was born at Twelveheads, not far from Chacewater. His family were miners worshipping in the local Methodist Chapel. At the age of 17 Billy went to Devon to work. Here he fell in with bad company, often getting drunk and fighting; he only just escaped jail. He was turned away from the mine where he worked for being insolent to the Mine

Captain and his drinking became so bad that he feared waking up in Hell!

After seven years away he returned home to Cornwall still continuing to drink heavily. His life was then turned around on reading Bunyan's Visions of Heaven and Hell. Billy was to become Cornwall's most noted miner-preacher. No other was so eccentric in the way that he addressed a meeting speaking their language with a joyful intensity. He would often illustrate his preaching with local experiences and incidents that the congregation could equate with. Billy would conclude meetings with, "Oh you Western Men! I am an old miner. Come to Heaven. If there is one crown short I will willingly go without one. But there is no want there. I tell ee it is a good thing to change a miner's hat for a crown."

While in the process of building one of his chapels almost single-handedly he wrote, "I was a very poor man, with a wife and five small children, and worked in the mine underground. Sometimes I was forenoon core (shift), and when I had taken my dinner I should go to the Chapel and work as long as I could see, and the next day do the same. The next week I should be afternoon cores; then I should go up to the Chapel in the morning and work until the middle of the day, and then go home and away to the mine. The week following I should be night core. I should then work about the Chapel by day and go to the mine by night, and had not the dear Lord greatly strengthened me for the work, I could not have done it. When I was about the Chapel, I had potatoes to 'teal' in my garden and every Sunday I was planned. I had to walk twenty miles and speak three times. I have worked twenty hours in the twenty-four."

Billy Bray's first chapel was in Twelveheads. His second was at Kerley Downs, near Chacewater – sometimes called 'Three Eyes' on account of its windows. The third, Great Deliverance, was built at Carharrack.

Examples of Billy's naive style of preaching include: "If God

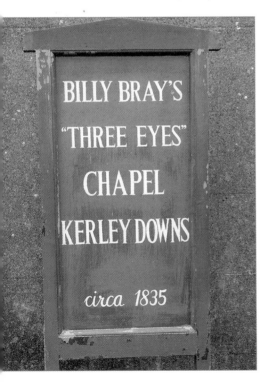

BILLY BRAY'S "THREE EYES" CHAPEL KERLEY DOWNS circa 1835

intended men or women to take snuff there noses would have been turned upside down." And "If the Lord intended men to smoke, He would have certainly made a little chimney at the back of the head for the smoke to pass through. But as He has not, I don't think He intended men to smoke!"

Look out for a little book called Billy Bray, The King's Son by F W Bourne, first published in 1877 and reprinted many times.

BROWN WILLY & ROUGHTOR

Brown Willy is Cornwall's highest point being 1375 feet or about 420 metres above sea-level on the granite Bodmin Moor. (q.v.) Why such a peculiar name? It is an Anglicised corruption of the Cornish Bronn gwennili – hill of swallows. Its neighbour Roughtor, pronounced 'Rowter' is English – rough crag. It is 1296 feet high or about 400 metres.

Visitor Folliott-Stokes wrote in the 1920's, "The steep slope of Roughtor is covered with great granite boulders dappled with lichens of the most delicate colour. The summit bristles with immense rocks piled one upon the other, a natural feature worthy of the gods. To the eastward, about a mile away, Brown Willy cuts the sky with its fine rugged outline, but it is not so rock-strewn as Roughtor. These two hills are probably more rugged and of a more mountainous character than any others of equal height in England."

BUDE

Surrounded by beauty but hardly a beautiful town. In 1899 Baring-Gould observed it to be "unpicturesque and uninteresting." Folliott-Stokes, in 1928, added that, "Bude is a difficult place to describe. It is such a disconnected collection of villas, portions of streets, and open spaces. Nothing in Bude seems to bear any relation to anything else." So much for the town which is functional in its purpose as a holiday resort, so let us concentrate on the beaches and the sea. Bude Haven is a refuge for boats in an area of Cornwall that has few harbours. A canal with lock gates to the sea was built between 1819 and 1826 originally working over a thirty mile range. Barges carried sand to inland farms for use as a lime-based fertilizer. The beaches are expansive and used by all from surfers to paddlers. One early visitor broke his leg and stayed until it was mended, writing long letters to his friends praising the pleasure of his rest, he was the poet Tennyson!

Another former resident was Sir Goldsworthy Gurney, one of the pioneers of steam road locomotives. Here he invented the Bude Light for illuminating lighthouses. He also proposed a differentiating flashing beam system by means of which each lighthouse could be identified by ships at sea.

C

CAMBORNE

Cam bronn, a crooked hill in Cornish. A mining town that is relatively young, having grown up in the 18th and 19th centuries. Before that time it was really just a village. Together with neighbouring Redruth tin and copper mines dominated the landscape. Camborne's most famous was Dolcoath, the Queen of Cornish Mines. It reached an incredible 3,500 feet depth before its closure in 1921. South Crofty, Cornwall's last working mine closed in 1998 but

with tin prices once again rising, could we see it fully working again? Never say never!

With the heritage of Richard Trevithick (q.v.) engineering was Camborne's mainstay. The world famous Holman Brothers Foundry, founded in 1807 was a large employer in the manufacture of industrial equipment from rock drills to compressors.

The Camborne School of Mines, famous as a hard-rock mining educational establishment, predating The Royal School of Mines by some twenty years, has had students from all over the World. It has now relocated to Penryn as part of the University of Exeter.

Trevithick's 1801 *Puffing Devil* road locomotive prototype inspired the song 'Going up Camborne Hill'. A song sung frequently, and not just by Camborne people, at various County functions. Every year, in April, Trevithick Day is proudly celebrated in the town with an emphasis on steam.

Musically Camborne Town Band have always been to the fore both within the county and beyond. So too are the Holman-Climax Male Voice Choir.

Camborne has always had a keen rivalry with the 'Choppers' of Redruth. The Boxing Day rugby match, probably the oldest rugby local derby match in the world, is vigorously contested and for some odd reason is termed a 'friendly match'!

CAMBORNE - REDRUTH TRAMWAY 1902 - 1927

Yes, Cornwall had trams! but for just 25 years and the only service was between Camborne and Redruth. The Redruth terminus was at West End where the waiting room and office still survive. It was The Urban Electric Supply Company Limited that undertook the works to join the two towns with Trelowarren Street's Commercial Hotel being the other terminus.

In the middle, at East Hill, Tuckingmill was the tram depot and the generating station providing power, not just for the trams but street lighting too.

Redruth historian Michael Tangye quotes from the West Briton, "On the 7th November 1902, Mrs. E B Beauchamp of Trevince opened the tram route by turning on the electric power to Redruth and Camborne, and at 3 p.m. it was opened to the general public. There were six trams, four double-deckers and two single.... with the price of two pence... it undercut the horse-buses and the G W R."

Complaints were made by cyclists, traction-engine drivers and horse-drawn vehicle users over problems with rails and the effective narrowing of the road. One unfortunate death occurred following an accident when a tram hit a blind and drunk inmate of the Workhouse at Barncoose.

With the introduction of motor-buses the demand for trams gradually decreased, the service being wound up in September 1927.

CAMELFORD

Ford, the English term, of the River Camel. Not the animal, despite the one on the Town Hall, nor even anything to do with Arthurian Camelot! The River Camel could well have the Cornish camm meaning crooked, but there is some doubt surrounding the name of the river with Alan being an alternative name.

Camelford is a small, and in many ways an insignificant market town some 700 feet above sea-level ideally situated for visits to Bodmin Moor. As a rotten borough it had two Members of Parliament up to the Reform Bill, one of whom was Lord Brougham. Not far away is Slaughter Bridge where a 9th century skirmish took place with the Saxons under King Egbert.

How ironic that the 1926 guide 'Cornwall, England's Riviera' should write, Camelford has "an abundant supply of pure water, and a good health record." For in July 1988 the water supply was contaminated when 20 tons of aluminium sulphate was poured into the wrong tank at the Lowermoor Water Treatment Works. Many people drank the 'poisoned' water, some with possible long-term health significance. Inquiries are ongoing to this day.

CHARLESTOWN

Unique to the county this is a privately owned historic working harbour. Designed by the celebrated John Smeaton, the harbour was begun by Charles Rashleigh in 1791. Rashleigh was a local squire with an interest in mining and the growing china clay industry. Until this time there was no ideal safe port in the St Austell area. Thousands of tons of rock were excavated, and to create a sufficient depth of water in the ba-sin, a leat was constructed from Luxulyan several miles away.

Shipbuilding, rope making and a foundry were all established within the harbour surrounds. Although at first the main export was copper ore, this was soon overtaken by china clay which dominated the port. Par and Fowey now have the bulk of this trade but Charlestown still does its bit. An extensive visitors' centre is a popular attraction as are the frequent visits of 'tall ships', some used in films.

That non-mincer of words Folliott-Stokes, writing in the 1920's found no beauty in Charlestown failing to recognise its industrial honesty when he wrote, "Its name should be changed to Little Hades. The smoke of its torment ascended

in heavy clouds of black and white dust as we scrambled down the steep hill-side into the gruesome pit, where a crowd of indistinguishable beings are forever emptying and loading an inexhaustible fleet of schooners. What the natural features of Charlestown originally were it is impossible to say, for everything is coated with white or black dust, sometimes both together, the result being a most depressing grey, as of ashes. Grass, trees, flowers, houses and people all share the same fate. How anyone can be persuaded to work, much less live in such a nightmare of a place, we cannot imagine." Possibly to earn a living?

CHINA CLAY

An industry based on the findings of William Cookworthy who in the mid 18th century tried to find an equivalent to the Chinese kaolin. He discovered the right clay on Tregonning Hill, near Helston, in 1746. China clay forms from a deep-seated chemical alteration of the feldspar in the granite – kaolinisation. The clay works remove the unwanted mica and quartz, the other main constituents of granite

The main area for china clay extraction is based around St Austell where the pits and spoil heaps are so familiar. The clay is obtained by mechanical methods, a very powerful jet of water is aimed at the decomposed granite rendering it into its component parts of quartz, mica

and clay. The sand is trapped and elevated to the spoil tips where some will be used for aggregates for the building trade. The milky liquid is run through mica traps where the kaolin is allowed to settle and later dried.

The main uses for china clay are in paper-making and surfacing, pottery and ceramics, fabrics, greases and soaps, paints and cosmetics. Some is used in medicines. Fowey is the chief exporting facility.

The three largest producers amalgamated in 1919 to form English China Clay Limited, holding 50% of the industry's capacity. In 1932 E.E.C. merged with rivals Lovering & Pochin to form E.C.L.P. But in 1956 the families of Lovering & Pochin were bought out to form E.C.C. International Limited who in turn were acquired by Imetal of France changing the brand name to Imerys.

CHOUGH

A member of the Corvidae – crow family, and has the name Pyrrocorax pyrrocorax. A black bird about the size of a jackdaw, with distinctive red legs and curved red beak, as depicted on the Cornish Arms. Although often misnamed the 'Cornish' chough, it is to be found in Wales, the Isle of Man, the Hebrides and the Irish west coast. An insectivore, it feeds on both adults and larvae, especially wireworms and leatherjackets, thrusting its long bill into earthy banks, either among short cropped grass or slaty rocks. An anthill is a special delight.

The call of the chough is described as 'kee-aw', similar to a jackdaw but softer. It has been suggested that the word chough might well have been pronounced 'chow', not unlike the sound of its call.

The decline and disappearance of the chough in Cornwall was probably due to a combination of factors. Some were trapped, eggs were taken as trophies and birds were kept as pets. These direct actions can be taken as only a part of the reason. Indirectly the bird has been a victim of the human colonisation of their environment. Ecological changes in agriculture, especially the less grazing by sheep and cattle of the cliff-top areas has led to rough plant growth and far less anthills. Perhaps the jackdaw is not without blame. Its increasing numbers has roughly corresponded with the chough's decline. Coincidence maybe, but man was enclosing more land and building more barns and houses, perfect for the nesting jackdaws who seemed to enjoy man's presence.

Around 1968 the last chough in Cornwall was spotted, that is until a few years ago. Not just cage-reared birds but real wild ones have once again appeared near the Lizard. It is hoped that this encouraging start may see a permanent return of Cornwall's emblem.

In Cornish folklore King Arthur (q.v.) is alive in the form of a chough.

CITY of TRURO,

The locomotive

Originally numbered 3440, the *City of Truro* is a G.W.R. City Class 4-4-0 steam locomotive. It was designed by G J Chuchward and built at Swindon in 1903.

It was almost certainly the first steam locomotive to pull a train at speeds of over 100 mph. While hauling the Ocean Mail from Plymouth to Paddington on 9th May 1904 two people independently timed its velocity at just over 100 mph. One was a postal worker on board the train who used a stopwatch to calculate the passing of the quarter mile marker posts. The other was a journalist for the *Railway Magazine* who was much more canny with his observations being familiar with speed record protocol. He later concurred with the speed being over 100 mph as was first claimed. This speed was attained while the train descended Wellington Bank in Somerset. This was at a time before any car or plane could achieve such a speed!

The *City of Truro* is now based at the Gloucestershire and Warwickshire Railway and still steams the occasional enthusiasts' train.

COASTAL FOOTPATH

Although the South West Coast Path is a relatively modern phenomenon with the 594 miles from Minehead to Poole being completed in the last thirty years or so, the need to walk the coast goes back centuries. Not walking for pleasure but with other motives in mind the coastal dweller needed to reach vantage points to observe fish movements, especially the migrating pilchards. Small hidden coves had to be accessed for 'wrecking' (q.v.) to retrieve much valued 'gifts of the sea'. Smugglers too would obviously avoid the main beaches and coves, and in their wake would come the Coastguard patrols treading the paths and frequently daubing marker stones with whitewash. As smuggling decreased so too did the number of cliff-walking patrols with a resulting increase in plant growth and a corresponding decrease in accessibility. Many of the early expeditionary visitors to Cornwall, who put their experiences in print, frequently rued their attempts at coastal rambling.

With greater leisure time and an increase in personal transport there came a demand to walk and explore the coast with a greater ease. Walkers wanted more challenge and to walk on new sections previously impenetrable. Towns and villages en route saw a new demand for bed and breakfast, pub meals and cafe service. Thanks to the local authorities and the National Trust the paths are now kept clear. Informative guidebooks even categorise sections into easy or challenging. Millions of pounds come into the Cornish economy as a result of this facility.

The coastal footpath is enjoyed by thousands each year. Serious walkers who march long distances, head down in all weathers, with an arduous schedule to keep. I sometimes wonder whether these 'route marchers' have time to appreciate the beauty and wildlife around them. "Look! A school of dolphins," I might inform, "Can't stop to look," might be the reply, "got to make Gorran by dark." Many of the walkers are short-course ramblers, often arranging drop-offs or pick-ups or devising circular excursions. Between these groups are a whole host of walkers doing things their own way and enjoying the Cornish Coastal Experience.

COPPER

Copper is a widely distributed element occurring in both combination and native (as the element) form. It has a fairly high melting point of about 1,100 degrees and is very ductile and malleable, and after silver, the best conductor of electricity.

There are a host of copper minerals, some with Cornish connections like Redruthite and Endellionite. Many different compounds produce minerals of ore quality, oxides like cuprite, sulphides like chalcopyrite and bornite, and carbonates like malachite or azurite. Ores carry only a low copper content – sometimes as little as 2%.

The most important use of copper is in the electrical industry. It is also extensively used in the manufacture of alloys such as brass (with zinc), bronze (with tin), and nickel silver (with nickel and zinc). Its salts are used in disinfectants, printing, dying, timber treatment and as a fungicide.

CORNISH LANGUAGE

Cornish is a language clearly allied to Breton, and to a lesser extent Welsh, Irish and Scottish Gaelic. These latter are further removed but are all tongues of the Celtic group of languages. The British Celts (Ancient Britons) who gave such resistance to the Roman invaders spoke a language closely akin to Cornish. Cornish was spoken throughout the county until about 1400. By 1600 English had pushed it to the west of Truro. It probably survived in the far west of Cornwall just into the 19th century despite the legendary Dolly Pentreath (q.v.) dying in 1777. Today Cornish is alive in place-names (q.v.) and as a field of study.

Little Cornish was printed before the start of the 18th century when Lhyud in his Archaeologia Britannica, 1707, published a Cornish Glossary and a Cornish Grammar, just as the language was dying out.

In recent decades much has been done to revise and 'tidy up' the Cornish Language and the complex mutation-rich vocabulary with a result that hundreds have reached varying degrees of fluency.

Dual-language road sign

A few Cornish words less frequently found in place-names:

ky = dog
melyn = mill
ruth = red
bugh = cow
margh = horse
pysk = fish
bowjy = cowshed
yeyn = cold
bryallen = primrose
poder = rotten
ledan = wide
hager = ugly

The UNESCO Atlas of Endangered Languages now deems Kernewek (Cornish) "critically endangered" and "in the process of revitalisation".

Cornish had gained official recognition under the European Charter for Regional or Minority Languages in 2002.

A number of schools have now introduced Cornish Language courses.

CORNISHMAN, OR NOT?

This subject of incessant argument needs to be aired. It is often said that to be Cornish one must have been born in Cornwall! But is it really that simple? What of the births of those from Cornish families who happen to live in the north and east of the county? The hospitals that serve them are either in Plymouth or Barnstaple. Try telling former rugby international Phil Vickery, born in hospital at Barnstaple, that he is a Devonian. Phil is from a family of Cornish farming stock living near Bude and is fiercely proud of his Cornishness. As to the argument of location of birth, Cliff Richard was born in India. Does that make him Indian? When eventually Man colonises Mars, will the first born there be a Martian? I think not! Don't forget the families of the Cornish exiles all over the world who are fiercely proud to be Cornish.

Perhaps it is a combination of many factors. To have been born in the county must help – so is the Prime Minister's daughter, born at R.C.H. Treliske, Cornish? It might be due more to feelings, emotions, love and a perceived identity. Possibly the length of habitation and a strong commitment to belong might have something to do with it.

CORNISH REBELLIONS OF 1497

In January 1497 Parliament voted for a tax to finance the campaign against James IV of Scotland. The Cornish, especially the tin miners who considered that their protection

The An Gof memorial
St Keverne

under Stannary Law (q.v.) was at risk, didn't like the idea that they might be at all interested in matters of the far away north. Led by Michael Joseph (An Gof – the smith) of St Keverne and Thomas Flamank, a lawyer of Bodmin, a small army left for London.

After a circuitous march, picking up the notable Lord Audley at Wells, some 15,000 armed, mostly Cornish men arrived at Blackheath in mid June. King Henry VII had sent an army north for the expected clash with James IV but these were recalled to London. The King's army had very little trouble in routing the rebelling army with possibly 1,000 of the latter being killed.

An Gof and Flamank were hanged, drawn and quartered as traitors at Tyburn on 27th of June. An Gof is reported to have said before his execution that he should have, "a name perpetual and immortal". Flamank said, "Speak the truth and only then can you be free of your chains". Audley, as a Peer, was beheaded.

The Cornish Rebellion had hardly threatened the Monarchy but did show the frailness of the political and social structure of England at that time.

A second Cornish uprising, in September 1497, was instigated by the pretender Perkin Warbeck who landed near Sennen with 120 men in two ships. Warbeck rallied the Cornish with promises of tax reductions and planned an attack on Exeter. At Bodmin Moor he declared himself to be King Richard IV and with much support some 6,000 entered Exeter and followed on to Taunton.

With news of King Henry VII's troops getting near, Warbeck deserted, later to be captured in Hampshire. The rest of the Cornish army surrendered. The ringleaders were executed and many fined. Perkin Warbeck was later hanged.

CORNISH REBELLION OF 1549

King Edward VI, the son of Henry VIII, being young and inexperienced was virtually dictated to by the powerful English nobles recently enriched by the spoils of the sacked monasteries. Huge Church reforms were announced most being unacceptable to much of the populace. The old Latin services were to be abolished and new ones brought in in accordance with the English Book of Common Prayer. Ancient festivals were outlawed together with the banning of images and certain ornaments. The Cornish were not at all pleased with this interference and rebelled.

During the summer of 1548 a King's Commissioner was stabbed to death while removing images from Helston Parish Church. In the following year some 6,000 Cornish armed themselves and under the leadership of Sir Humphrey Arundell of Lanherne and Boyer, the Mayor of Bodmin, marched up country. While they basically had a loyalty to King Edward, their threatening grievance was, "We will not recyve the new Service because it is but lyke a Christmas game, but we wyll have our olde Service of Mattens, masse, evensong and procession, in Latten, as it was before. And we the Cornyshmen, whereof certain of us understande no Englyshe, utterly refuse thys newe Service." Other demands were made concerning ceremony. It is clear that many of the Cornish at that time could not speak English but used the Celtic Cornish language. A take it or leave it response from the King to the petition sparked the rebellion.

A protest march began with the Cornish being joined by others from Devon which took siege of Exeter. After fierce fighting over several days the rebels were defeated. As a consequence Arundell was executed in London. Boyer was taken back to Bodmin where he was hanged.

An unusual account is told about John Payne, the Mayor of St.Ives. When the King's Commissioner reached the town he ordered that a gallows be erected. He then invited Payne to dinner at The George and Dragon Inn. After the meal the Mayor enquired of the hanging only to be told that it was for him! A similar tale is told of Boyer, the Mayor of Bodmin.

The new prayer book was brought into use replacing the old Latin one. Possibly, had the new prayer book been translated into Cornish, as it was into Welsh, the Cornish Language might have had a much longer life.

CREAM

Before fridges were commonplace in homes, Mother would scald (simmer) any of the fresh milk that was left over on the day to keep some usable milk for the next morning. The resultant crusty rich top that was skimmed off was what we called cream. On a larger scale on the dairy farms milk was allowed to stand for twelve hours in the summer months, and for up to twenty-four hours in the winter. During this period the natural cream rose to the surface. Pans would be slowly heated over a fire until the cream showed a raised ring around the edge. When the scalding was sufficient the pans went back to the dairy and stood for another twelve hours to allow the firm yellowish crust to settle to become clotted cream

For some reason certain people want to drag up the Phoenicians as a factor in the origins of clotted cream in the same way that they want them to be responsible for saffron cake. (q.v.) There is really no evidence or even logic in this thinking. Cornwall was supposed to have traded with the Phoenicians with tin, but why they would have knowledge of dairying to the extent of teaching the Cornish to scald milk is nonsense!

Modern production has necessitated certain changes. At Cornwall's leading creamery, Rodda's of Wheal Rose, 200,000 litres of milk are used a week. A centrifuge speeds up the long settling process of former times as well as producing a safer and longer lasting product. Rodda's supply not just this country, but their cream may be sampled on planes during international air travel!

Now for more controversy. Is there a difference between Cornish clotted cream and the Devonshire equivalent? No, not much anyway, but there is in the cream teas! In Devon traditionally scones are used as the base, but in Cornwall it was always a split – a rounded soft bread roll. You can argue all day as to whether it is jam on top or cream. It is easier to put the jam on first, but most people justify their method as truly Cornish on the grounds that that was what Granny did!

One more thing – thunder and lightning! That is a split or slice of bread with treacle (golden syrup) and cream. Again it is easier with the cream on top, but watch what Granny does.

D

DAVY, SIR HUMPHRY

Sir Humphry Davy's statue may be seen at the top of Market Jew Street in Penzance. Educated here he first developed a love of poetry – in fact Coleridge once said that had he not devoted himself to science he might have become one of our great poets. At the age of twenty he went to Bristol being an assistant to a Dr Beddoes. Here he made experiments with gases, dangerously using himself as a guinea pig to test their effects. Nitrous oxide, laughing gas, was his next field of study.

He became Secretary of the Royal Society in 1807 and its President in 1820. He separated the alkaline metals, showed the nature of chlorine and by using electrolysis separated water into hydrogen and oxygen. Davy introduced the Voltaic Arc and his experiments on vegetable physiology were the beginnings of Agri-chemistry. He was succeeded by his brilliant pupil Faraday. Some cynics say a discovery equal to his many others!

Davy is best remembered for the invention of the miner's safety lamp. An oil lamp which was enclosed by a wire gauze allowing air to feed the flame but excluding the inflammable gases that were present in coal mines. Prior to the Davy lamp many terrible explosions occurred causing death and injury to thousands. It was typical of Davy's humanity that he took out no patent for the device. It has been pointed out however that less caring mine owners used the benefits of the lamp to push miners into more dangerous situations – a result that would have left Davy aghast!

DELABOLE

One of the largest holes in the ground in the world is at Delabole. Padel tells us that the name is the obscure Deli with a pit – bol which dates back to the 1280's. The pit was a slate quarry and is therefore over 700 years old.

The slates are Upper Devonian in age and well described by Carew in his Survey of Cornwall, 1602, as being "in substance thinne, in colour fair, in waight light, in lasting strong." All qualities that meant it was in great demand. It was estimated that two and a half million cubic yards were extracted by the mid 18th century. Other quarries were opened to extract this high-quality roofing slate. By World War II the

31

main quarry was an oval 40 acres in extent and 410 feet deep. It employed about 350 people.

Cornwall is not well blessed with fossils but at Delabole there is a fascinating one. It is a brachiopod, Spirifer verneuili, that has been crushed into a double kite shape. The bivalve sea creature, originally round, has been transformed into a 'butterfly', the wings each a valve, known locally as a 'Delabole Butterfly'.

DIALECT, ACCENT & STRESS

Dialect is the use of words particular to the county. Many will have Cornish Language origins, some true to it, others slightly modified with time and place. The use of dialect has diminished and will continue to do so with modern publications and the very strong influence of the national media, together with population movements and the recognition of the written word. Remember that universal literacy is a relatively recent achievement.

Dialect tends to vary from parish to parish. An example from fishing vocabulary is the name for a spider crab. Cornish 'gevryk', it is called gaver in Portloe, while just a few miles west at Portscatho it is a gavrik. No doubt other Cornish fishermen have different yet similar names. The garfish, Cornish 'gerrak', is still named garrick or gerrick in many places.

Mining too was a rich source of dialect words. The guttering that catches the rain from the roof, to a Cornishman, is a launder, a term from tin-streaming operations where stream water was led through wooden channels called launders. Geologists accept the word killas for our local slate rocks. It comes from the Cornish 'kyllas'.

Farming, the countryside and cooking all provide a rich source of dialect words; shiver – the wooden bar of a farm gate, aglet – haw, fruit of the hawthorn, slab – the cooking range. It can be seen that dialect not only included Cornish Language words, but alterations in standard English pronunciations. A fisherman may go to 'say' (sea) and may catch 'wan' (one) or two!

One of the writers who studied the Cornish ways of speaking during his stay at many locations was Charles Lee. Although a Londoner, A.L.Rowse felt that he caught the dialect and speech mannerisms better than any other. Sir Arthur Quiller-Couch hailed him "a writer who could use our (Cornish) speech as we use it, and understand our ways generally." Charles Lee's Cornish Tales, Dent 1940's, is well worth seeking out, as is his collection Chasing Tales, edited by Simon Parker in 2002. An example with my translation comes from his journal of 1898 written in Portloe. "A man at Trewartha got drunk and scat up the cloam. So next day his wife gave him a sherdy pasty for croust." A man at Trewartha got drunk and broke the crockery to bits. So next day his wife gave him a pasty made with the shards of china for his lunch.

One of the criticisms often heard about the portrayal of the Cornish accent on television and radio is that "they never get it right!" Come on, think about it. There is no one Cornish accent. Listen to a man from Bude and compare it with the singing lilt of a St Ives man. A man from Redruth says that he is from reDROOTH, but his neighbour from Truro insists he is from REDruth! Falmouth is similar to Truro, while St Austell is close. Don't disparage the different accent just because it is not anything like your archetypal slant.

Finally, that word 'dreckly' (directly), Cornish for at a time in the future, but I'm not sure exactly when. (the late M.P. David Penhaligon (q.v.) even used it in the House).

But, say the knockers, directly literally means straight away. Yes, I reply, but you use the word presently – and what does that literally mean? At present, or in other words now! I rest my case.

DUCHY OF CORNWALL

This dukedom was introduced by King Edward III in 1337 to provide support for his eldest son, Edward the Black Prince who in 1346 at just 16 years of age fought at the battle of Crecy. After Prince Edward predeceased the King, the dukedom was recreated for his younger son who was to become Richard II.

Since 1503 the eldest son of the Sovereign has inherited the title, Duke of Cornwall, with land totalling c.52,000 acres in Cornwall, Devon (including Dartmoor Prison), Somerset and London (including The Oval cricket ground).

If the Duke of Cornwall should die, then the eldest son will not inherit the title.

EDEN PROJECT

Situated in a former china clay pit near St Austell, the Eden Project is an internationally famous and much respected attraction based on the relationship between plants and Man.

The whole concept was formulated by Tim Smit who had been the driving force behind the successful Lost Gardens of Heligan. Here he and his team transformed an overgrown classic Cornish garden into a first class visitor attraction. With others, including architect Nicholas Grimshaw, together with leading technical experts, they were able to produce a plan to construct huge biomes of a futuristic nature.

Opening in March 2001 visitors were welcomed to a landscaped attraction including the world's largest 'greenhouse' – The Tropical Biome – nearly 4 acres of computer controlled humid environment growing bananas, coffee, rubber, etc.. A smaller Mediterranean Biome is nearby. The structures are based on tessellated hexagons and pentagons forming a steel framework for the plastic cushion 'lights'. Temperate outdoor areas surround the biomes which have been used for concerts and filming James Bond in Die Another Day.

Recently a new facility, The Core, has been built as an educational provision with classrooms and exhibition spaces. In November 2010 Eden was able to overcome severe flooding to continue as an exceptional Cornish institution.

EMIGRATION OF CORNISH MINERS

The tin mining industry attained its highest point in the middle of the 19th century. Since that time a slow but steady decline took place leaving derelict workings, desolate mine dumps and skeletal engine houses in almost every parish. The skilled hard-rock miners sought to continue their trade in other parts of the World taking with them an expertise unparalleled in any other country. From 1850 to 1900 the population of England and Wales doubled while that of Cornwall showed a marked decrease. During that period almost a quarter of a million Cornish left their homeland for good!

Peruvian silver mines first saw Cornish engineering expertise with Trevithick's (q.v.) pumps installed in 1816. The 1830's saw Redruth and St Just men directing operations and native labour in the Cuban copper mines, while the 1849 Californian Gold Rush tempted many, as did discoveries in Australia. Many Cornish ports saw the send-offs of miners charged with optimism and some degree of trepidation, many on their own with a view to sending for their families when they made good, others taking the bull by the horns and risking the whole family's future.

Nicholas Penhaligon and Bill Trebilcock, each with a small bundle of possessions, tramped from Carrigan Downs to Padstow and sailed to California. After three months they landed at a log cabin village called San Francisco. In 1850 the *Clio* sailed from Malpas, near Truro, with passengers for America. Regular weekly services were established from St Ives and Hayle to the ports of Bristol and Liverpool, between Falmouth and Fowey to the ports of Plymouth, Southampton and London. All of the thousands of emigrants would then cross in larger ships to their hope-filled destinations.

Some returned home to Cornwall having made some money, but many never came back, leaving 'Cousin Jacks' living all over the mining countries of the world. In 1870 miners were travelling from Cape Town to the newly discovered diamond fields of Kimberley. This was followed by gold on the Rand and the Transvaal. There were 'Cousin Jacks' at Johannesburg when the city was in its infancy. For several years, near its centre, was the well known Cousin Jacks' Corner where Cornishmen would congregate on Saturday nights.

From 1890 to 1900 special coaches were added to the up-trains from Penzance, labelled Southampton, the embarkation point for South Africa. There in the Joubert Park would be hundreds of Cornishmen, but because of the terrible working conditions, as well as typhoid, many would succumb to phthisis, a form of miner's lung, few would live beyond forty. But the allurements were strong, £8 per week at home would be £80 in the goldfields!

While Cornishmen were flocking to America, Australia and South Africa, they were in smaller numbers making for mining camps in many other parts of the world. Zacchaeus from mid-Cornwall raised nine sons, the lives and deaths of whom are shown below:

William went abroad at 20. He returned home, a grey-haired man of 55, then disappeared again.

Dave died in New Zealand.

Ki travelled the world for 30 years and came home to settle.

Jerry died in Montana.

Wazzy died in Australia.

Luther left as a lad and never came back.

Johnny died at home of African phthisis.

Martin was killed at Bendigo, Australia.

Willie, the greatest traveller of all, made a small fortune and went to live alone in his late father's cottage.

Today there are descendants of these Cousin Jacks all over the mining world, many still fiercely proud of their Cornish roots. It was said that wherever in the world you find a deep hole, you would find a Cornishman working at the bottom.

Redruth miners at Johannesburg, c.1895. The authors great-grandfather, Frederick Simmons, second in the middle row, died of phthisis at the age of 46. None survived to old age!   The Authors Collection

F

FAL, The River

The source of the River Fal is on the Goss Moor at Pentivale (Head of the Fal) near Roche. It flows through Grampound and Tregony where it soon meets tidal water at Sett Bridge near Ruan Lanihorne. The Ruan River section silted up owing to the large amounts of china clay waste that not so long ago turned the river a milky white. By Tregothnan Boathouses the Fal joins with the Truro River to flow past Tolverne and through King Harry Passage. So, despite a popular misconception, the Fal does not go anywhere near Truro or Malpas!

Further south past Turnaware Bar the estuary widens to form the Carrick Roads. Here is one of the finest natural harbours in the world. Delightful creeks that branch off the Fal estuary include Coombe (for Kea plums) and Cowlands, Pill, St Just (q.v.), Restronguet (Pandora Inn), Mylor and Penryn. Both Tolverne and Turnaware were extensively used in the preparations for the Normandy landings.

North of Turnaware Bar in the deep narrowing section of the River, on either side of the King Harry Ferry (q.v.) many huge ships can be seen in a 'laid-up' state.

The number of ships is considered to be an indicator of the state of world trade.

In the Carrick Roads during the winter months oyster fishermen work silently in their traditional sailing boats or rowing boats. Dredging by wind or muscle power is the only method allowed in this conservation conscious ancient fishery.

Because it drains granite moorland the Fal is regarded as the most radioactive river in the country.

FALMOUTH

A town of 17th century origin is the usual claim, but Padel has found a reference to a Falmouth Villa in 1478, and a William Falmouth in 1403, thus indicating that a small settlement of Falmouth did exist. There certainly was a Smethick in 1370 and a Pennycomequick in 1646, two sites that some believe grew into the town.

The growth of Falmouth owes very much to the Killigrew family's interest at the beginning of the 17th century. Up until then Truro and Penryn were the chief ports. In 1670 the Customs' House Quay was built, quickly followed by other waterside developments enabling

Falmouth to become a packet station. The Post Office ships carried not only mail, but passengers too, firstly to Spain and Portugal and later to North and South America including The Caribbean. The P.O. eventually handed over the service to the Royal Navy in 1851 resulting in Falmouth's loss and Plymouth's gain. However Falmouth's reputation as a maritime centre had been established.

The railway arrived in the 1860's giving a boost to the town. I wonder if things might have been different if the line from Truro had been dual with a consequent rise in prestige for Falmouth. Ship building and repair soon boosted the once fishing based marine economy with the dockyard later to become dominant employing thousands of men. Tourism and pleasure boating were soon to become evident with impressive hotel building taking place overlooking the Bay. For the commercial shipping Falmouth has become a major bunkering port.

A well presented Maritime Museum is a must visit attraction.

FARMING

The development of farming is dependant upon many factors, social and economic as well as geographical, geological and climatic. The far west of Cornwall already had enclosures as the Celtic field system grew from the need to manage the large numbers of loose

granite rocks. Much of the rest of the County became enclosed with the need to control stock, both to be kept in and to be kept out.

Cornwall's soils vary, especially in respect of the higher moorland. Cyrus Reading in his Illustrated Itinerary of the County of Cornwall, 1842, said Cornwall has "sterile hills and granite peaks, extended wastes, and districts boasting a fertility surpassed nowhere in the islands." On the whole the soil, especially over granite, is acidic, but the close proximity of the sea enabled limey beach sand to be used as a soil dressing as well as seaweed as a fertilizer.

Demands for food crops were at first almost solely local, so cereals – wheat, barley and oats were widely grown in areas that today we would consider to be unfavourable. Potatoes were cultivated in a battle with the then difficulty of controlling disease in our warm, moist climate.

According to Worgan in A General View of the Agriculture of Cornwall,1811, Cornwall was surprisingly not a dairy county, with the modest amounts of milk, meat and dairy products all for local consumption. Soon the better farms raised larger breeds of cattle, in particular the North and South Devons. "A large white long-sided, razor-backed pig was the true Cornish breed," said Worgan. The pig was so ubiquitous that as late as 1859 there were 170 such animals within the bounds of Truro! Sheep

were mostly found in the hillier districts. Relatively few horses were kept for riding, being mostly used for ploughing and hauling. Oxen were surprisingly common in Cornwall, a pair doing all that horses could do, but more slowly. At the end of the ox's working life there was also meat to be had!

One of the major influences on farming was the advent of fast transport, especially the railway. Counties could now specialise in what they did best, that is to use their soils and climate to advantage. Less wheat was grown, other parts of the country, or even the world, being better suited. The better suited dairy and early crop industries really took off. There was a growing and easily accessed up-country market to be serviced with early vegetables and spring flowers produced ahead of the growers further north. There followed a move away from the small mixed farm to larger specialised farms with a massive adoption of machinery. Socially the army of farm labourers consequently dwindled creating a population change within the countryside and a whole new farming scene.

Today there is much contract growing whereby, for example, supermarkets agree to purchase crops or produce of a standard quality. This is especially true of winter and spring vegetables such as cauliflower and potatoes, as well as milk and to some degree beef.

The first years of the 21st century proved difficult for farmers with incomes much reduced and certain animal diseases proving hard to control. However there has been some recovery since, but with an industry so reliant on weather and possible climate change, not to mention the vagaries of economics, the future is never certain.

FISHING

Man has fished the sea for thousands of years, but preserving the catch was always a problem. Salt was not easy to come by, although there were some 'saltworks' mentioned in the Domesday Book, most fish was sun-dried. By the 13th century deals with France were made which resulted in an easier access to salt and better equipment. In return the French were licensed to fish off Cornwall. From this time the Corn-

Lobster pots

wall and Devon fishing industry grew to become of national importance by Tudor times.

By the second half of the 16th century it was believed that Cornwall had a fishing population of 2,000 with some vessels venturing as far as the coast of Ireland. Locally the main fishing was for pilchards, both for home consumption and for export. But almost beyond belief were the trips taken 400 years ago while braving the Atlantic. By the early 17th century as many as 200 Westcountry boats were engaged in the Newfoundland cod trade. Fishermen signed on for a period of two summers and a winter away of hard toil, often at the mercy of pirates as well as the cold.

Following the all important pilchard fishery, it was the herring that came next. Local boats, as the fish got more scarce, would go to the North Sea to continue their trade. They would continue around the Scottish coast and head south to the Isle of Man, always chasing the herring. The entire journey would take some three months.

Mackerel fishing was important, especially in Mount's Bay and St Ives Bay, but gradually the competition from larger boats, both British and foreign, made its mark. Their size, coupled with steam power, was difficult to match.

The coming of the railways altered the fishing scene. Fresh fish instead of salted could now be quickly sent to new inland markets. At this time, and up to 100 years ago the Cornish fishery employed over 1,000 local men. But at varying seasons these would be augmented by up to 1,000 French who would take their catches directly home. Inshore many crab and lobster fishermen plied their trade.

The second half of the 20th century saw massive improvements in technology using radar to find fish, together with the development of larger and better equipped vessels. This efficiency, however, saw the numbers of boats and men sharply decrease in an age of tighter regulation. The need to conserve stocks was accepted by most, but the methods and the acceptance by all the fishing nations, would lead to conflict. The targeted fish species could only be caught in accordance with strict regulation by quota. The throwing away of over-quota fish, no matter how marketable, leaves a bitter taste in the fishermen's mouths. Decommissioning of vessels and limited days at sea all come in for criticism, but a system that is agreeable to all may prove to be impossible.

See the section on pilchards.

FITZSIMMONS, BOB

Bob was born in Helston on 26th May 1863, the twelfth child of a policeman and his wife. In the 1870's they emigrated to New Zealand, together with other Cornish families, to Timaru. Bob's father, James, set up as a farrier employing his son who quickly developed the skills of a smith and at the same time developing great upper-body strength.

It is thought that Bob's first boxing match, a bare-knuckle fight, was against a huge local blacksmith. Fitzsimmons, although only fifteen and weighing eight and a half stone, won in the first round! A few years as a 'jobbing' boxer in Australia were followed by a move to America in May 1890. Within a year Fitzsimmons had established the right to fight for the World Middleweight Title. At the age of 27 he showed outstanding qualities of stamina being able to absorb punishment and back it up with a mighty hitting power. He fought Jack Dempsey in a fight to the finish, but with

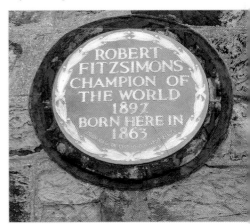

Fitzsimmons' birthplace,
Helston

41

a maximum of 45 rounds! After 14 the unbeatable Dempsey was pummelled to defeat.

The famous lawman Wyatt Earp refereed the fight against Tom Sharkey. With Bob easily winning, Earp disqualified him with the accusation of a punch while Sharkey was down. Many believed that Earp was in cahoots with a large betting syndicate.

Fitzsimmons had in his sights 'Gentleman' Jim Corbett's World Heavyweight crown, but Corbett dodged a showdown many times. Corbett's indecision resulted in his retirement leading to a match for the vacant title. Bob Fitzsimmons was up against Peter Maher in February 1896 in a fight that would be the first to be filmed. However Bob won within 95 seconds well before the cameras were rolling. But with the untrustworthy Corbett denying his retirement, Bob's title was declared void. Eventually public opinion demanded that the contest take place.

The day was 17th March 1897, the place Carson City, Nevada. After a few rounds the heavier Corbett was clearly ahead, knocking Bob down in the 6th. Encouraged by his wife shouting, "Go for his body!" the fight began to turn. Round 14 and Fitzsimmons landed his famous 'solar plexus' punch. He advanced, dummied a punch to the chin, Corbett raised his guard and Fitzsimmons was in. Corbett failed to beat the count and Bob had won.

His title was lost at the first defence, but there was yet more to come. In 1903 the 40 year old Fitzsimmons was challenged by the 26 year old Light-Heavyweight Champion, George Gardiner. Despite winning on points after 20 rounds, the next day Bob collapsed with pneumonia. He recovered and continued to box for a few more years eventually dying from the disease on 22nd October 1917.

'Ruby' Robert as he was known was described by Cornwall based author Winston Graham in his short story 'Jacka's Fight', 1971. "Fitzsimmons was no figure of a boxer at all. You would laugh, and many did, for already he had a bald patch and had long arms and legs like thin poles quite out of proportion to his great chest and stomach. He weighed scarcely more than 150 lbs (10stone 10) and had a red round face, and his teeth were large and bright like wet tombstones and had stood all the unkindness of the ring. He would have done proud as a comic turn in a circus but it would be foolishness to take him seriously as a boxer."

To have held three different World Championships at the old well-spaced weight divisions was unparalleled.

FOWEY

A very busy port now, especially for the export of china clay, and a very busy port in the Middle Ages for mixed cargoes. At the time of Edward III (1327 - 77), Fowey

sent more ships to the Royal Navy than any other port. The town quickly climbs up the hill from the estuary in a haphazard fashion, while looking across the water to the villages of Polruan and Bodinnick. Walking through the main street fascinating glimpses of the harbour appear, disappear and reappear at frequent intervals. Perhaps the best way to experience the real Fowey is from a boat!

Folliott-Stokes in his The Cornish Coast and Moors, 1928, writes in his inimitable style, "The visitor is confronted with a coup d'oeil that leaves an impression not easily effaced. At once he is intimate with the life of the town, and coming and going of the ships, the rich verdure of the enfolding hills, and the beauty of their inmost recesses, revealed by the sinuous windings of the river. Live a week or two in Fowey, and you will find the charm of it all grows upon you."

Sir Arthur Quiller-Couch immortalised Fowey in a series of books about 'Troy Town'. It also became the home of famous writer and lover of Cornwall, Daphne du Maurier.

G

GARDENS OF NOTE

The greatest of Cornish gardens are at their unbeatable best in the Spring. Renown for magnolias, camellias and rhododendrons, which include azaleas, the climate is usually kind enough to encourage an early show of colour. Sub-tropical plants abound with bamboos, tree ferns and many palms.

The gardens of Caerhays Castle, overlooking the sea near Gorran, hold a national collection of magnolias including some of record size. The home of the Williams family, who with others did a great deal to sponsor the intrepid 'plant hunters' in their search for new species, and who gave their name to the Williamsii camellias first bred at Caerhays and being especially suited to Cornwall. There is an extensive and well stocked woodland garden that is a must to visit.

Mount Edgcumbe House on the Tamar opposite Plymouth has a national camellia collection in spacious grounds.

Heligan, the Lost Gardens, was cleared and developed in 1992 under the direction of Tim Smit (see Eden Project), John Nelson and John Willis. The original gardens were abandoned at the start of World War I when the men got called up to fight. There is a Victorian productive area, Italian and Alpine features, with traditional and wildlife sections.

Glendurgan (National Trust) is situated in a sub-tropical valley on the Helford River. It has an impressive maze set in a very attractive garden.

Trelissick (National Trust) is situated on the Fal Estuary near the King Harry Ferry. It has an excellent collection of plants with scenic walks making it especially attractive at all times of the year.

Trengwainton (National Trust) is near Penzance with a walled garden. It is able to grow some good examples of exotic species.

On the Helford is Trebah, also in a sub-tropical valley, and quite close to Glendurgan. It has a good display of spring and other seasonal plants. In a period of just over twenty years Trebah has grown into a major attraction.

Trewithen, near Probus, east of Truro, is the home to the descendents of the Hawkins family who were also sponsors of the 'plant hunters'. It has many specimen plants and a wide selection to impress all.

Tregothnan, home of the Boscawen family, overlooks the Fal

and is an historic, typically Cornish spring garden. Together with many specimen plants it is experimenting with tea growing and production – tea plants are a type of camellia!

There are many other good gardens of varying sizes having impressive plant collections. The National Gardens Scheme organises the opening of dozens of notable small gardens all over the county.

GEOLOGY

Cornwall is basically a tableland out of which rise a number of granite hills. The former is composed of ancient rocks, the oldest being the complex serpentine and other igneous rocks of the Lizard. To the north of these are bands of slates mainly of Ordovician age, and about 400 million years old. In Cornwall the mix of slates is generally termed killas.

At the end of the Carboniferous period, about 340 million years ago, the West of England was the scene of great crustal movement resulting in the intrusion of a great mass of acid molten material (magma) cooling under the old rocks to form a granite mass from Dartmoor to Scilly. After consolidation the volatile components of the magma came off as vapours and solutions along fissures penetrating the rocks, altering them and depositing metallic lodes, these later being exploited in mining.

Few deposits are found of a later geological age. Some fossils may be found in the east of the county, but these are few and far between.

There have been many times of sea level changes, resulting in varying wave-cut platforms leaving the granite (q.v.) as 'islands'.

The geology of Cornwall is unique being unsurpassed in mineral variation with abundant tin, copper, arsenic, wolfram (tungsten), lead, zinc and even uranium, all offering the chance of commercial extraction. To see one of the finest mineral collections in the world you must visit the Royal Cornwall Museum at Truro.

In the relatively recent tilting of the county along a southwest - northeast axis the submergence of the south coast has led to drowned valleys (rias), as at Fowey, Falmouth and Helford. These contrast with the emergent north coast's magnificent heights where little streams have had to cut their way down through hundreds of feet of killas, such as at Porthtowan and Portreath.

GIANTS

The giants have left their marks on the hills of Cornwall. The granite areas especially show their washbasins, baths, punchbowls, hand and footprints as well as the stone stacks where they played.

St Michael's Mount was built by the giant Cormoron and his wife

Cornelian. The former was friendly with the giant of Trecobben Hill. In fact they shared a cobbling hammer which they would throw to each other as required. On one occasion the hammer was thrown to the Mount striking Cornelian fatally on the head. There are many other stories relating to Cormoron.

The giant Bolster persecuted the blessed St Agnes until she was compelled to a plan to destroy him. It was said that Bolster could stand with one foot on St Agnes' Beacon and the other on Carn Brea some six miles away! How he managed when needing short steps we are not told. Bolster was known to take a new wife each New Year and his monstrous existence troubled the village. Agnes tricked him into a blood-letting to improve his health and appearance and so make him a realistic suitor for her. With the bung removed from the basin in the cave at Chapel Porth he bled to death staining the sea red.

Many other giants lived in Cornwall and should you wish to delve more deeply, I suggest Popular Romances of the West of England by Robert Hunt, 1864, and Cornish Saints and Sinners by J Henry Harris, 1906.

GOONHILLY DOWNS

Goon is Cornish for downs, but hilly is uncertain and definitely not of the English meaning. Situated in the centre of the Lizard peninsula it is an S.S.S.I. – a site of special scientific interest. Its flora is suited to its geolo-

gy, serpentine for the most part, with talcose slate, steatite and the basaltic greenstone. Of special note is the Cornish Heath (erica vagans), recently voted to be Cornwall's national flower, as well as some rare legumes.

From a distance the Downs are dominated by the presence of technology. From 1962 a satellite earth station was developed with its distinctive dish aerials. The first to be constructed was *Arthur*, of open parabolic design, some 26 metres in diameter and weighing over 1,000 tonnes. It received the first live television broadcast from America on 11th July 1962. The transmission only lasted for a few minutes until the satellite, *Telstar*, orbited beyond the horizon. The largest dish, *Merlin,* has a diameter of 32 metres. The telecommunications set-up was, until recently, open to the public, but now the whole operation has moved to Hertfordshire with Goonhilly mothballed.

However exciting new proposals are being put forward in 2010. B.T. have sold a large section of the property to a consortium which includes the University of Oxford.

It will work with defence technology firm QuinetiQ and the U.K. Space Agency to turn the former telecommunications hub into a world class space science centre.

GORSETH KERNOW

Without doubt going back hundreds of years, the Cornish Gorseth was revived in 1928 at a time when there was a growing interest in all things Cornish. It was modelled to some degree on the ceremonies of our Celtic cousins in Brittany and in Wales. The first of the revivals took place in the Bronze Age stone circle of Boscawen-Un in West Cornwall where once, no doubt, ceremony was commonplace. Since then the Gorseth has travelled the county from Zennor to Liskeard. The meetings are based on the natural Cornish spirit, encouraging the study of language and history, supporting literature, art and music, and encouraging trans-Celtic links. The Gorseth ceremony is impressive with the Bards dressed in blue robes with rituals spoken in Cornish.

G Pawley-White, a past Grand Bard, summed up his passion in the 70's with these lines, "Have the flowing blue robes, the sounds of the Cornish gwalas and the harp and the ceremonies conducted in a once defunct language any place in the seventies? The robes, as do academic robes, certainly play a picturesque and colourful part in the ceremonies, the sound of horn and harp are more pleasant than many of the sounds which afflict our ears elsewhere; and the language is recognised as an essential part of the Cornish heritage. There will always be a place in the life of the community for the beauty and colour of pageantry and spectacle. The real worth of the College of Bards, however, is done not in the Open Gorseth... but in the continuing work of the members in the various organisations they serve... Gorseth Kernow will continue to foster the progress of the culture of Cornwall, to enrich the common life in the development of resources latent in the Cornish people and to encourage peace and friendship amongst all people... Kernow, Cres ha Kerensa – Cornwall, Peace and Friendship."

GRANITE

Granite is an igneous rock formed in a molten state. It consists mainly of three minerals: quartz, mica and feldspar. The intrusion of the masses of magma which formed the granite areas of Cornwall, about 300 million years ago, was responsible for the mineralization both within the granite itself and the surrounding altered slates (killas). It was these metal ore veins that enabled mining to evolve.

Cornwall has four main bosses of granite – Bodmin Moor, St Austell Moor, Carmenellis and West Penwith. Around these are smaller outcrops such as Kit Hill and Kingston Downs, St Dennis

and Castle-an-Dinas, Hensbarrow, Carn Marth and Carn Brea and Tregonning and Godolphin Hills. Even smaller ones are at Cligga Head, St Agnes Beacon and St Michael's Mount. All of these outcrops, together with Dartmoor in the east and Scilly in the west, are joined at some depth.

Underground changes to the granite during the process of crystalisation in certain conditions – pneumatolysis – altered the rock to form china clay (kaolinisation) especially, but not solely, in the St Austell area, leading to a major industry. Granite is and was extensively quarried in Cornwall. Each area produced rocks of different type and appearance, its strength and durability being highly desirable qualities for buildings, bridges, piers, lighthouses, etc.. The coloured and decorative forms are used for monumental work.

HALSETOWN

Halsetown is only a little hamlet west of St Ives, but I include it because of its unusual raison d'etre.

John Halse, 1769 - 1838, was a Truronian who became M.P. for St Ives. His development, Halsetown, was carefully planned with the occupying tenant miners each having just the minimum amount of land to qualify for the vote! Each tenant was of course a John Halse supporter. A visit to the 'town' will show the calculated arrangement of cottages, each in its own plot.

Halsetown, like some other Cornish towns and villages, had a mock mayor-making ceremony. The elections would take place on the same day as the real ones in St Ives. At the 'council meeting' the usual nonsensical motions were put forward, for example that Halsetown would be lit by gas. When the mockery was completed adjournment was made to the inn for feasting and drinking to the new 'mayor'.

HAYLE

Cornish for estuary – heyl. As a port Hayle has always had its problems with the sand bar at the mouth of the estuary. But despite this the Cornish Copper Company made improvements by building a wharf at Carnsew with a canal cut to Copperhouse in 1769. Land was acquired by John Harvey in 1779 for a foundry, while his son Henry later dredged and deepened Penpol Creek in 1818 to take larger ships. A regular packet steamer service to Bristol was added in 1831. Harvey's developed strongly with the foundry, mining supplies, dry-docking and ship launching facilities. Large ponds of sea water were trapped at high tides and

later released at low water to flush the channels. Harvey's became very powerful using their own ships to import pig-iron and coal for the foundry which made large steam engines as well as a wide range of other products. They almost monopolised local trade by including in their business general stores, furnishing, inn keeping, farms, mills, building supplies and coal. They made over 500 Cornish Engines for mine working, many being sent all over the world.

Transport was improved with the Hayle causeway construction in 1825, prior to this the road went through St Erth village. An alternative was to take the low tide route across the sand to Lelant. The steamer service to Bristol was very active with St Ives M.P. John Halse preferring it as part of his home journey from London, this in 1836. Coaches were still slow and uncomfortable.

The sea always supported a small fishing fleet as well as the steamer and freight trade, while Hayle had its own lifeboat from 1866 to 1920. Up to the demise of the small coal-fired power station, the estuary was dominated by such a generator, the coal being brought in by sea. A new renewable energy (q.v.) project involving wave power has its site a few miles off shore.

Gradually Hayle has developed its holiday potential completing a move from industry to tourism. For details of this progression see 'Tourism'.

The further development of the town has been held back by a succession of rash financial promises over the past twenty to thirty years without any visible show of progress in the harbour area. Surely it must be Hayle's turn soon?

HEAVY CAKE

There is a debate within the county as to the correct name for this slab of cake. Heavy cake, yet it is certainly not heavy, or 'hevva' cake from the Cornish word 'hevva' – the shoaling of fish, especially pilchards, near the surface. Cyril Noall, a much respected St Ives historian, was certain it was the latter. The women made 'hevva' cake "to celebrate the payment of their allowance after a successful enclosure (a seine net of pilchards). This was composed of plain flour, lard, sugar and dried fruit, the dough being rolled out in sheets, like pastry, marked in a criss-cross diamond pattern with a knife, and baked in the slab." (a Cornish range)

As for the debate, I'll go with Cyril!

HELFORD RIVER

"You might think the Helford River is much like any other. You would be wrong to think so. It is the one Cornish creek where the kingfisher is unremarkable. When you have done gaping at it and at the loveliest creekside village in England – Helford – and finished playing darts with the yachting folk in one or other of the ideal pubs at either end of the ferry, you begin to consider the problem, how best to leave, if at all possible to leave the Helford River." So wrote J.R.A. Hockin in his 'Walking in Cornwall', 1936.

Helford was once a busy little port in the 18th century exporting tin ore and also having a fishing fleet. Later a stone quay was added to cope with more general cargoes. However the steep access to and from the port was a deterrent to hauliers, especially at a time of horse power. Now the village is dominated, like so many other coastal villages in the county, by the second home owner whose occupancy is in no way long enough.

The river has a history of being a quiet haven for those involved in piracy and smuggling. This, an inspiration to Daphne du Maurier to set her adventure story 'Frenchman's Creek', the location being known locally as 'Pill' – Cornish for a little inlet. The preservation of the estuary's natural scenery was due in no small part to the Vyvyan family of Trellowarren who were the primary landowners keeping a tight control on human development.

Durgan and Trebah have wonderful gardens and were embarkation sights for the D Day landings by the American troops.

Pass the bar, the famous cockle-picking area, to find Port Navas (Porth Navas) which has the Duchy Oyster Farm. Helford oysters are renowned, but a few years ago problems arose from a disease normally only found in the Pacific.

At the head of the estuary is Gweek, once a tin ore exporting port and since the 14th century a port for Helston, cut off by the Loe Bar. (q.v.). It still has some marine activity including a boatyard.

HELSTON

The 11th century name Henlistone, according to Padel, shows the origin of the name Helston to be Hen Lyn – ancient court plus the English ton – town, and not the tempting Hayle's town – town on the estuary. Its first charter from King John was in 1201 when Helston was a small port on the River Cober handling ores of copper and tin. It is thought that it was in the 13th or 14th century that the Loe Bar (q.v.) had grown sufficiently large to prevent all but the smallest craft from joining the sea. Helston became a Coinage town with Stannary duties under a charter of Edward I. The Coinage Hall stood near the centre of Coinage Hall Street.

The town has become famous for its Flora Dance, more correctly a 'furry' dance, the word coming from the Latin 'feriae' – a festive holiday. Flora is a relatively modern term. The dances, traditionally held on the 8th May, are performed to a familiar and repetitive tune played by the Brass Band. The dance with its simple routine goes around the town and through the houses. Couples dress in finery with the men in top-hats and tails, the women in long dresses. The leading couples consider it a great honour to be invited to dance, all true Helstonians dream of the occasion. A children's dance also takes place.

With an early start, the Hal-an-tow ceremony begins. Spring flowers and greenery are collected and the town is decorated, lily of the valley being especially prominent. A procession walks the streets accompanied by the beat of a drum and fife band, together with the pealing of the church bells. The Morning Song is sung which includes the following lines:

With Hal-an-tow, jolly rumble, O,
For we were up as soon as any day, O,
And for to fetch the summer home,
The summer and the May (may), O,
For summer is a-come, O,
And winter is a-gone, O.

In a combination of May Day and the day of St Michael, the green shoots of spring are welcomed, in some ways like Padstow's celebration the early pagan ideas of the spirits of nature are at the basis of 'furry' day.

Near Helston is the extensive RNAS Culdrose. Established in 1942 it has become a vital helicopter base for the Royal Navy as well as providing search and rescue services. Helston is proud of its association with Culdrose and is very thankful for its economic benefits.

HMS CORNWALL

The present *HMS Cornwall* is a type 22 frigate, the sixth Royal Navy vessel to be given the name. She was built by Yarrow Shipbuilders and launched on the Clyde by Diana, Princess of Wales in October 1985. She was later commissioned by her, I like to think as the then Duchess of Cornwall, at Falmouth three years after. She carries the Cornish badge of fifteen gold bezants with the motto 'One and All'. Not however in Cornish, but in the Latin 'Unus et omnes'. Among those to whom there is an affiliation are the County of Cornwall, The Cornwall Rugby Football Union and The Cornwall Royal Navy Association.

Some data:

5,300 tonnes displacement
487 feet long
48 feet beam
21 feet draft
250 - 300 ship's compliment
18 knots cruising speed
30 knots maximum speed

The ship is to be de-commisioned.

HOGS' PUDDING

A very tasty and essentially Cornish pork sausage-like preparation. Eaten as it comes, that is cold after boiling, or shallow fried – delicious! Occasionally, in former times, the blood of the pig was added to make 'bloody pudding' but that must have been a bit too much like black pudding. You don't see it now. Comparisons of hogs pudding are usually based on texture and above all, on the herbs that are added. Recipes used by the most appreciated makers have normally been handed down over generations and are guarded like the Crown Jewels. People often swear by the puddings that they grew up with, so if you are from Redruth you would have gone for Bartles, and from Truro it would have been Crowle and Moss.

A recipe from the Cornwall Federation of Women's Institutes, 1929:

Clean some pig skins, and let them soak in salt water. Take fresh pork, lean and fat, put through the mincing machine, then add breadcrumbs, thyme, salt and pepper. Mix all well together, take skins out of water, dry, and stuff with the mixture tightly, then tie up each end. Boil until cooked.

HURLING

A rough and tough sport, a kind of hand football played between teams of men, sometimes representing town and country. As well as in Cornwall, it was played in Celtic countries like Wales, Scotland, Ireland and Brittany. In Cornwall especially a silver ball was often used, a cricket ball sized sphere of cork, wood or leather with a thin silver outer covering. Some of the early balls carried inscriptions relating to acceptable play, for example, "Fair play is good play." (Guare wheay yu guare teag.)

In his Survey of Cornwall, 1602, Carew describes two kinds of hurling. Firstly, hurling to goal, "mostly used at weddings where the guests took on all comers.". Secondly, and far more ferocious, was hurling to country where the event could run for miles to a predetermined goal. Carew explained, "In the matches the hurlers take their next way over hilles, dales, hedges, ditches, yea, and thorow bushes, briers, mires, plashes, and rivers whatsoever, so you shall sometimes see twenty or thirty lie tugging together in the water, scrambling and scratching for the ball."

Feast days were the usual times for the parish hurling. The contests were hard and long with no quarter asked or given. A.K. Hamilton-Jenkin in his Cornish Homes and Customs, 1934, informs, "A visitor enquiring if a game was likely to be a good one, is said to have received the stark reply, 'We have every reason to believe so, there's a lot of bitter feeling between the two teams!' " I see parallels here with

St Columb's Silver Ball craftsman, Colin Rescorla

the modern 'hurling' rugby matches between neighbouring towns!

During the reign of Charles II, Cornish hurling was staged in front of thousands in London.

In West Cornwall St Ives were top dog, taking on teams from St Buryan, Sancreed and Sennen. St Ives and Lelant had been keen rivals, but as the populations grew so unevenly, the latter could no longer compete. The silver ball was therefore kept at St Ives.

Around 1870, according to *The Western Morning News*, "Hurling took place annually on the Feast Tuesday at Tregony. The tollgates at Grampound Lane and at Golden forming the goals. The married men took on the single, as was the custom at Truro".

Today hurling is contested in the old style at St Columb where it is town against country. At St Ives the hurling is now for children only with the silver ball being thrown up by the Mayor on to the beach at Lambeth.

I

INDIAN QUEENS

This village is included to represent the settlements within the County that grew up around inns. Bugle, London Apprentice, Victoria and Crowntown are some of the others. The Indian Queen was not unknown as a pub name having been found in Altarnun and Gwennap, the latter having Queen Victoria, the Queen of India, on its sign.

The inn at Indian Queens was called the Queen's Head in 1780, later changing to the Indian Queen. Eventually on its closure the licence was transferred to the nearby St Columb Road inn, to become the Queen and Railway. The sign-board of the old inn once displayed a Red Indian on one side with Victoria, Queen of India on the other. These were painted over when the inn became Dean's Temperance Hotel.

There is no logical reason to believe that it was the Red Indian Pocahontas that was the 'queen' in question. She did arrive at Plymouth in 1616 but travelled directly to London never ever visiting Cornwall. Although not proven, the Indian Queen in question is almost certain to have been Victoria.

ISLES OF SCILLY

Scilly has place-names of Cornish language origins. Its geology and archaeology are very similar to Cornwall. It shares its health and police services but it is not a part of Cornwall!

K

KING HARRY FERRY

This is a vehicle carrying ferry crossing the Fal Estuary and linking Feock (St Feock) with Philleigh on the Roseland. In 1888 The King Harry Steam Ferry Company Limited was formed with a capital of £2,000 in £1 shares, with a plan to replace the old man-powered craft with a steam driven one. Since then there have been many improved vessels taking vehicles to the Roseland, especially for St Mawes, and back. It is in a delightful location and was recently voted one of the best scenes anywhere!

As for King Harry, there is no record of King Henry VIII ever having been in the area despite some people's romantic notions. Cornish historian Charles Henderson had the most likely explanation. The river passage was named after King Harry, that is Henry VI. On the Philleigh side were the remains of a tiny chapel mentioned in 1528 as 'The Chapel of St Mary and King Henry'. It commemorated Henry VI who was murdered in 1471 becoming known as 'King Henry the Martyr'.

L

LANDER, RICHARD & JOHN

At the top of Truro's Lemon Street stands a monument commemorating the explorers Richard and John Lander, natives of the town, being born at the Fighting Cocks Inn. In his short life Richard made three expeditions to Africa where he traced the River Niger to its source, at the same time trying to generate trade. Unfortunately he was the only one to survive. Undaunted he set out again in 1830 accompanied

by his brother, and this time tracked the Niger to its mouth, During his third expedition he was attacked by natives and died of his wounds.

LAND'S END

An English term of course for this most westerly point of mainland Britain. Never locally accepted in the past as a significant bit of cliff, Cape Cornwall was considered to be the tip of the county by many in West Cornwall. While the people to the east at Porthgwarra Cove had residential claims of a geographical nature of their own.

Land's End may not be the most spectacular Cornish promontory, but it does have an undoubted atmosphere, provided of course that you keep looking out to sea and not turn around! Views of the Longships' Lighthouse and beyond to Scilly, in good visibility, both add to the cliff's granite splendour. You may, if you wish, imagine the legendary lost land of Lyonesse (q.v.) somewhere out in the deep.

J.R.A. Hockin in his Walking in Cornwall, 1936, puts it well, "Land's End can hardly have acquired much of its magnetic force before our regrettably objective tourist age. If anything Cape Cornwall always seems to me the more fitting end than 'one of the least interesting points on the coast', but Land's End beats it by about half a mile, and the desire to shudder over what for us islanders has something of the morbid fascination of the End of the World and to consummate the conclusiveness of Cornwall is irresistible."

Yes, as a Cornishman, I went there once because I suppose I felt that I ought to. I haven't been back in the forty years since because I fear that I might be upset at the thought that our county's end is now in title only as a secondary attraction to the man-made visitor bit!

LAUNCESTON

Let us begin with the controversy of its pronunciation. Some say Lawnston, some say Lanson. Perhaps the origin of the name will help. Padel tells us that the original name was Lann Stephan, the church site of St Stephen, with the English tun (ton) for an estate added later. In his Cornish Place-Names, 1988, he tells us, "In 1086 and earlier it referred to St Stephens, across the valley, and not to the present town: that had the English name of Dounhed, 'hill end', now revived in the archaic form Dunheved. In 1155 the canons of St Stephens moved across to what is now Launceston, and the name was transferred also." He shows that it was pronounced Lanson in 1478. So the first part of Launceston is Cornish for church land or a church site – lann. So is that not how we should now pronounce it? Of course those of us brought up in the west of the county have been ingrained with 'lawn' and find it hard to change our ways. We won't worry about the Tasmanians! Perhaps we should accept that the way to pronounce a place is to copy the pronunciation of the majority of the natives.

Launceston was Cornwall's main town in the Middle Ages with an important castle. Until 1835 it was the County Town, relinquishing to Bodmin. The castle was home, in the 13th century, to Henry III's brother Richard, Earl of Cornwall. During the Civil War it saw action and after changing hands several times, ended up Royalist.

A guide of the pre-bypass 1950's describes the town, "However Launceston is approached its antiquity is apparent. 'Foreigners' from England driving down the great A30 highway climb the long hill up from the Tamar to the narrow streets and turn a sharp corner to find an old town gate bottlenecking the traffic. Narrow streets beyond open into the centre of the town, a steep enclosed triangle under the walls of the Castle, and in the blink of the eye one can see the old medieval market place."

My Grandmother would describe a miserable situation as "like Lanson Gaol". The town's lock-up was described in an official report as being in a most filthy and dilapidated state. There was no water, no privy and no exercise yard. When the Keeper was asked about fresh whitewash he said that it was to be left as dark as possible like a real gaol. There was a fireplace, but no fuel!

LEVANT MINE DISASTER

Levant tin mine is in the West Cornwall granite area not far from St Just and Geevor. Perched on the cliff-top, many of the working levels ran out under the sea.

Firstly we need to go back to 1841 when The Royal Cornwall Polytechnic Society offered a prize for the best idea for a machine to raise miners to the surface. Something needed to be done to overcome the inefficient and strength sapping ladder climb that could take up to 45 minutes at the end of a laborious shift. Engineer Michael Loam's design for a 'man-engine' was the winner. Basically it used the 12 feet rise and fall of the engine's beam to raise a rod fitted with small platforms moving between equally spaced fixed ledges, By stepping on and off the miners could be lowered or raised with little expenditure of energy. Some 'man-engines' employed a double rod for even speedier travel. This simple labour-saving device was

surprisingly slow to be introduced with only eight installations in the county by 1862.

Levant's 'man-engine' was described as 'ancient' in 1917 by miner Raymond Harry (see note below), with the main shaft having no cage as in most other mines. The 'man-engine' was believed to be the last working anywhere in the world. The rod reached down to the 266 fathom level, about 1,600 feet below the surface.

On the 20th October 1919 miners getting ready to ascend stood on the sollars (ledges). Others, especially the younger ones, started climbing the ladders to get on at a higher level. A little later quivers were felt in the rod's motion. The younger miners at the higher levels took no heed and soon reached the top. But there were no more miners following. After a deafening noise a shout went up, "The engine is gone!" The rod had become detached from the beam taking with it the miners on the platforms down to the 100 fathom level (600 feet) where everything jammed.

Rescue attempts were made, some access being made from the shore. Thirty-one miners died that day. The whole of the county was in shock, with the waves of grief reaching the rest of the mining world.

Try to obtain a copy of the little book, The Mine Under the Sea, 1962, by Jack Penhale, whose real name was Raymond Harry, the miner mentioned above.

LIFEBOATS

At the time of writing Cornwall has seven large all-weather vessels, stationed at Fowey, Falmouth, The Lizard, Newlyn (Penlee), Sennen, St Ives and Padstow. Some are kept afloat, others are slipway launched and one is tractor towed. Many inshore 'ribs' are to be found, not just at the major stations, but at many intervening places along our coast. But it was not always so. In the days of rowing and sail-assisted lifeboats many more were needed to cover their slower passage. In fact, from Falmouth eastward there were once five lifeboat stations: Portloe, Mevagissey, Polkerris, Fowey and Looe. Most of the Cornish stations were founded between 1850 and 1870.

The introduction of motor lifeboats enabled greater distances to be covered. A change in the nature of the casualty has also taken place due to the huge growth in pleasure boating and a lesser demand from the

commercial. It is in the former area that the inshore boat comes into its own with its state of preparedness, speed and manoeuvrability.

Cornish seafarers have always proudly worn the R.N.L.I. jumper, risking their lives to help those in trouble. Generous with their contributions the Cornish people have always been keen to boost the essential funds needed to maintain this charity based organisation. The stories of three lifeboat tragedies follow:

Within a year St Ives suffered two disasters. The first on 31 January 1938 when the 3,700 ton steamer *Alba* attempted to reach St Ives Bay but fell short crashing on to the north-west side of The 'Island'. The lifeboat, *Caroline Parsons*, was launched with Coxswain Thomas Cocking, reaching the lee of the *Alba* and dropping an anchor so that she could use it to pull away from the wreck. The *Alba*'s crew of 23 were helped into the lifeboat, which itself had a crew of nine. As the *Caroline Parsons* got away she was hit broadside by a huge sea which turned her over throwing most into the sea. Although self-righting, the lifeboat was unmanageable and was swept on to the rocks with a few survivors clinging on. Five of the *Alba*'s crew were lost.

A replacement boat was sent to St Ives, the *John and Sarah Eliza Stych*. A year later on the 23rd January 1939 she was launched in response to a report of a ship in danger near Cape Cornwall. Soon after 2 a.m. the lifeboat rounded The 'Island' in tremendous seas. Thomas Cocking was again at the helm when the boat capsized. The self-righting boat came up again, but this time without four crew members, including the Coxswain. Rescue attempts were thwarted by the failure of the engine to restart, so an anchor was dropped and a red flare fired. The anchor cable broke and the lifeboat drifted helplessly in the gale. She rolled again and this time only three remained. By now the boat was nearing the rocks at Godrevy. Once again there was a capsize and now only one, William Freeman, was left. He managed to scramble ashore.

The town mourned the Coxswain and his son, as well as two brothers from the seven lost. The ship that started the whole affair was never identified, but bodies were found at Gurnard's Head.

On 19th December 1981, the coaster *Union Star* was on her maiden voyage from the Netherlands to Ireland with a cargo of fertilizer when she got into difficulties a few miles from the Wolf Rock. Without power due to the fuel having been contaminated with sea water she first turned down help from a tug with worries over the compensation claim that would follow. The crew of four plus the Master were accompanied by the Master's wife and two daughters, especially to be together at Christmas. Eventually, with the gale now reclassified as a hurricane, a distress signal was sent. But by now the *Union Star* was close to shore near Lamorna.

The Penlee Lifeboat, *Solomon Browne*, a wooden 47 ft. Watson craft was launched with a crew of eight, all from Mousehole. Twelve crew had mustered, but only one from each family were allowed to go. Coxswain Trevelyan Richards and his crew reached the casualty and skilfully got four off. The second approach proved fatal. There were no eyewitnesses but both vessels may have rolled on to the rocks. Three other lifeboats, together with helicopters were summoned, but could do nothing. All sixteen were lost with only eight bodies being found.

The village of Mousehole mourned, as did the whole of Cornwall, and still on the 19th December each year, the Christmas lights are turned off in respect.

LIGHTHOUSES

Cornwall's first lighthouse was erected at the Lizard in 1619 by Sir John Killigrew of Falmouth. Passing ships, in theory, paid a fee to fund the enterprise. Later the responsibility for and the funding of all the lights fell to the Brethren of Trinity House, London.

The earliest structures were scaffold mounted or more substantial towers with keepers' cottages nearby. Rock-station lighthouses were extremely difficult to build with the more exposed bases only being accessible a few times a year when weather and tides allowed. The Eddystone Reef saw its first structure erected in 1698, followed by a succession of improved models including Smeaton's now on Plymouth Hoe.

1795 saw the Longships built off Land's End with many following in the 19th century including the Wolf, Pendeen, Godrevy, Trevose and St Anthony. One 20th century example is the modern Tater Du Light between Penzance and the Land's End.

There is one lightship based at the Seven Stones Reef where the Torrey Canyon (q.v.) came to grief. All Cornish lighthouses are now operated automatically

LISKEARD

The name is from lys, Cornish for court, with probably the personal name Kerwyd (Padel).

Liskeard is a genuine market town at the head of the Looe valley It was the headquarters of the Royalists during the Civil War (1642 - 8). There is a large church second only to that at Bodmin.

In 1828 a canal was opened running for five miles from Moorswater below the town to near Looe. It started by bringing sand and lime inward with farm produce out. It later carried copper ore from the Caradon mines. In 1860 the canal was replaced by the scenic Looe railway, a must for visitors to the port.

Godrevy Lighthouse

LIZARD, The

The mainland's most southerly point named from the Cornish lys – ardh, court on the high ground. With the exception of Lizard town itself, the area is unique in both geology and scenery. Its cliffs and beaches are outstanding and its villages are of great interest. But because of its remote location away from the dominant N.E. to S.W. county alignment, it is often overlooked.

The geology of the Lizard is complex and unlike the rest of the country. The rocks are crystalline and metamorphic, that is they have been highly altered by pressure and heat. The famous serpentines are just some of many of The Lizard rock types. The peninsula has some distinctive flora including the Cornish heath on the moors and samphire on the coast. Its fauna has now once again been enriched by the return of the chough.

The western settlements include Gunwalloe, Mullion and Kynance. The first has a fine beach with an associated church with a detached tower. Mullion village is a little inland from the cove, while Kynance has the much painted serpentine cove of many shapes and colours.

At Lizard Point is the powerful lighthouse 230 feet above the sea, throwing its flash of light every three seconds and seen for 21 miles. In Polpeor Cove is a former lifeboat house used before the present Kilcobben site housed the Lizard-Cadgwith vessel. Nearby Landewednack is a must to visit.

On the eastern coast is the pretty village of Cadgwith, and separated by sandy coves, valleys and headlands, Coverack is another delightful fishing hamlet. On the coast near the substantial St Keverne are the two villages of Porthallow and Porthoustock, the latter being an exporter of roadstone.

"One goes to the Lizard to live in the open air, to battle with the strong sou'westers, and to draw health and strength from contact with Nature where she is still rugged, primitive and lusty. And one can find all this either along the many miles of indented coastline, or on the central plateau – Goonhilly Downs (q.v.) which rises to nearly 400 feet above the sea level." So says a 1926 guide, Cornwall, England's Riviera. Says it all, doesn't it?

LOCAL RADIO

Until the early 80's Cornwall and Devon were served by just a few regional programmes on the B.B.C. including 'Morning Sou' West'. But in January 1983 B.B.C. Radio Cornwall started to broadcast with a mix of music, news, sport and general interest themes. It was a service that was well received. A weekly news bulletin is now in the Cornish Language. Many personal-

LOE BAR AND POOL

The Loe Bar prevents Helston from being a port at the head of an estuary. It is composed of sea-polished pebbles, mostly of flint and chert. A bore-hole drilled in 1834 through the gravel reached 68 feet without finding a bottom. Another drilled in 1859 just a quarter mile south of Helston passed through 33 feet of alluvium, indicating a once tidal port. The pool (the loe) formed in the 14th century when the bar was substantial enough – it is now more than 150 yards wide. The fresh water would slowly percolate through the pebbles in times of modest rainfall. But in the winter the River Cober would overfill the pool with resulting floods in lower Helston. Today there is a culvert on the western side of the bar which allows the water in the pool to remain at a constant level, but it was not always so.

The lake and the adjoining land belongs to the Penrose Estate. With the town of Helston threatened and the working of the mills in peril, a curious ceremony was enacted. A bag containing three ha'pennies would be offered to the Lord of the Manor for permission to cut the bar. The request was always granted.

The bar has a flora and fauna of its own including many rare maritime plants and a moth found nowhere else.

ities have emerged, each with their own broadcasting slant. Lawrence Reed's award winning phone-in programme in the early afternoons has become a firm favourite. While Duncan Warren and Pam Spriggs have also featured on Pirate FM. Many other regulars have given the broadcaster a friendly, feel-good, and local flavour.

1992 saw the start of Pirate FM, a commercial broadcaster aiming at the young and not quite so young across the county and into Plymouth and West Devon. The output is popular music, avoiding the more obscure, with regular news and sport updates. Pirate FM have always been a leader in high tech radio.

Atlantic FM started in August 2006 from St Agnes, it too being a commercial broadcaster. With an audience target of between 25 and 54 they entertain with contemporary music and news.

Source fm caters for the community of Falmouth and Penryn.

LOGAN ROCK

There are many logans, which should be pronounced loggans, in Cornwall. These are large rocks that have naturally weathered to a point where they can easily be rocked. The most famous logan is the one in St Levan parish at Treryn Dinas not far from the Minack Theatre.

This Logan Rock is about 90 tons of granite, "so evenly poised, that any hand may move it to and fro, but the extremities of its base are at such a distance from each other, and so well secured by their nearness to the stone which it stretches itself upon that it is morally impossible that any lever, or indeed force (however applied in a mechanical way), can remove it from its present situation." So wrote Borlase in his Antiquities of Cornwall, 1754.

Now there was a challenge if ever there was one! Enter a young Lieutenant Hugh Colvil Goldsmith, nephew of the famous poet Oliver, of the preventive cutter *HMS Nimble*. *The Gentleman's Magazine*, 8th April 1824 reported, "A party of sailors...... commanded by Lieutenant Goldsmith, came on shore for the purpose of removing from its situation that great curiosity the Logging Stone, and which object they were unfortunately enabled to accomplish." Goldsmith had landed with 14 of his crew and attached handspikes and a jack, eventually dislodging the famous rock by manpower alone.

There was much local outrage resulting in a meeting of The Admiralty. Goldsmith was ordered to reinstall the rock using capstans and whatever else was needed from Devonport Dockyard. He had also to forfeit his commission.

On 2nd November, before a large gathering, The Logan Rock was hauled back into place. But the balance was never the same. It is now very hard to move at all.

LOOE

An East Cornwall fishing and holiday town split by a tidal river estuary into the larger East Looe and the smaller West Looe.

West Looe was originally called Porthbyghan, little harbour, and it still is the sleepy side of town. East Looe, like some other Cornish seaside towns, has many narrow streets with little back alleys. But above all Looe is the river and the sea.

Up to the Reform Act of 1832 the rotten borough of Looe sent four M.P.s to Parliament. During a pre-vote debate one Member declared that, "There is only one borough more rotten than East Looe, and that is West Looe!"

At one time a canal brought minerals from the Liskeard area to the port being replaced in 1860 by the railway. Gradually the tonnage became too much for the port to handle and it became solely a fishing harbour. The train still runs from Liskeard and I strongly recommend leaving your car at the former and entering Looe in comfort and style.

Today Looe is highly regarded for the quality of its fish owing to the boats working on a daily basis so ensuring fresh catches to the market. The town has an inshore lifeboat station and a peculiarly shaped pier, appropriately called the Banjo Pier. If you encounter a local be sure to greet him with, "Hello Mr Pengelly." You have a good chance of being right!

LOSTWITHIEL
It always puzzled me that the little settlement of Withiel, near Bodmin, wasn't the one that was lost like the town in question. I should have realised that the name Lostwithiel does not start with the English 'lost', but with the Cornish for tail. Withiel means forest or wood, so Lostwithiel is the tail of the wood.

A truly historic town with its first charter being granted in 1196. There is a little bit left of the Duchy Palace, a 14th century building, used as an Exchequer, Shire Hall and Stannary Prison. Cornwall was ruled from here under the patronage of the Earls, followed by the Dukes of Cornwall. The prison in 1805 noted a debtor who was allowed access to a grated window where he could beg with a shoe hanging from a cord to avoid him from starvation!

It was a major port for tin ore but declined from the mid 14th century due to the silting up of the River Fowey's upper reaches caused in no small part by tin streaming further up. Lostwithiel's loss was Fowey's gain, the latter developing strongly.

In 2010 the town suffered serious flooding with the swollen river threatening the impressive 15th century bridge.

LYONESSE, THE LOST LAND
The legend says that Lyonesse united West Cornwall with the Isles of Scilly. That it was a fertile land occupied by the Silures, a righteous and God fearing people who enjoyed the use of 140 churches. (A later commentator, after some logical thought, believed that there couldn't have been more than 40!) The inundation by the sea was recorded as in 1090 and according to the Saxon Chronicle, on 11th November! The sole survivor was supposed to be a Trevelyan riding on the back of a swimming horse. Some say that at certain tides and conditions you can still hear the church bells and choirs singing in the stalls.

It is true that the Scilly Isles were once fewer in number but covering a larger area there being an extremely gradual inundation over thousands of years. Similarly St Michael's Mount was once surrounded by trees. But taking the average age of parish churches in Cornwall to be 600 to 700 years, it just doesn't add up. However there is land in two places in the divide. The Wolf Rock and The Seven Stones Reef.

M

MANACLES, The

A group of rocks, extremely dangerous to shipping, between Falmouth and The Lizard. This area has probably seen more shipwrecks than any comparable location in the South-West, apart from Scilly. The origin of the name is probably Cornish, with meyn meaning rocks and eglos meaning church. So meyn eglos became manacles over time. It may be that their sharpness suggested church steeples, although these are not common in Cornwall, or is it a reference to St Keverne Church as a landmark when viewed from the sea?

The death toll from this notorious group of rocks is over 100 ships with nearly 1,000 people drowned.

The most notable wreck was that of the *Mohegan* on 14th October 1898. All of the officers in charge of the steamship died in the disaster leading to many questions that cannot be answered as to the cause of the loss. She left Tilbury on October 13th with 53 passengers, a crew of 97, 7 cattlemen and a stowaway, all bound for America. Only 44 out of the 158 souls were to survive.

The *Mohegan* was reported as ten miles from the Eddystone Light at 5 p.m. on the 14th, but from that sighting the remaining hours of her life are a mystery. For some reason her course had been set at west by north and not west by south which would have taken her 10 miles south of Falmouth. At Falmouth, eyewitnesses saw her some miles off making course adjustments. At Porthoustock, the Coxswain of the Lifeboat was aware of a light in a dangerous position and immediately summoned the Lifeboat's crew and they were soon underway. The Coverack Coastguard was also sufficiently alarmed to send up a warning rocket.

On board the *Mohegan*, at 6.50 p.m., a slight shock was felt in the engine room, this being the beginning of the end for the ship. With the ship's telegraph put to 'stop' water was already coming in through the rents in her hull. Very quickly the water level rose and soon put a stop to the dynamos, leaving the ship in darkness. Captain Griffiths ordered the lowering of the lifeboats and everybody to don lifebelts. Four distress rockets were fired from the bridge, but by now the ship was three-quarters awash and listing sufficiently to prevent the launch of the starboard lifeboats. Within minutes the *Mohegan* was totally awash.

The Porthoustock Lifeboat rescued many from the ship's lifeboats and got the survivors ashore. At 8.45 p.m. the Falmouth Lifeboat, escorted by a tug, was called out together with Cadgwith and Polpeor (Lizard) Lifeboats, but were too late to save more than one person. The Porthoustock Lifeboat returned to take off a further seven from the rigging. After further searches she returned to base at 5.10 a.m. Coxswain Hill was later to receive the R.N.L.I. Silver Medal. A mass grave at St Keverne Churchyard holds the bodies of most of those who perished. A simple stone cross stands there with the one word on it – *Mohegan*.

MARCONI AT POLDHU

Guglielmo Marconi (1874 - 1937) was an Italian inventor best known for his work to devise a radio telegraph system. Together with Braun he shared the Nobel Prize for Physics in 1909 for contributions to the advancement of wireless telegraphy.

Why then is he in a book on Cornwall? Following years of experimentation he was ready, in 1901, to attempt a trans-Atlantic radio signal link-up. He chose the cliffs above Poldhu on the Lizard Peninsula to be the transmitting location, hoping to be heard at Signal Hill in Newfoundland, a distance of 2,200 miles. Many towers were erected at Poldhu in order to send the Morse Code letter 'S', constantly repeated, on 12th December

1901. At Newfoundland a 500 foot high kite supported aerial was to be the receptor. That the first radio signal to cross the Atlantic was received was never independently confirmed. It was reported to be so faint as to make it almost impossible to differentiate from static! However, Marconi and his company continued to pioneer radio telegraphy for many years.

MEBYON KERNOW

Mebyon Kernow – Sons of Cornwall – was founded in Redruth in January 1951. At first it acted as a political pressure group but later became politically active in its own right. MK's main objectives include establishing greater autonomy in the county through the establishment of a legislative Cornish Assembly.

In 2010 Mebyon Kernow had 18 elected representatives – 3 on Cornwall Council and the others in town and parish councils.

At present MK is, "Cornish, Green, Left of Centre and Decentralist."

METHODISM

The Methodist Movement originated with the brothers John and Charles Wesley. While the two were at Oxford they formed a club in which members promised to work and study religion regularly. John's actual words included "they resolved to live by the rules and method", hence Methodists.

They wanted to take the word of God to all parts of the country and, above all, to reach all classes of people. On their first visit to Cornwall in 1743, they received a great deal of opposition. Only a few clergymen appreciated the fervourous wake-up call of the Wesleyans and offered encouragement for their preaching.

The Wesley brothers were of course real clergymen of the Church of England, but unlike their parish-bound colleagues they preferred to spread their message far and wide. John's own diary records him at Gwennap at 5 a.m. and at Stithians at 8.00 a.m. He then went to Wendron, preaching under the shade of a tree at 2 p.m. At 5.00 p.m. he was at Crowan before riding to St Ives in the evening! The party relied on blackberries from the hedgerows and commented on the lack of hospitality with, "Do the people think that we can live by preaching?" In reality the growing numbers of his followers were poor and hungry themselves.

John Wesley visited Cornwall about forty times and with each visit his popularity grew. Meetings were so greatly attended that few meeting rooms were large enough to accommodate the throngs necessitating outdoor preaching. The Wesleys, not being particularly tall, would often find a large rock to act as a pulpit. One such boulder is at the foot of Rosewall Hill near St Ives.

The best known meeting place, and a must to visit, was Gwennap Pit, a few miles from Redruth. An excavation from mining work it was sculpted into a perfect open-air amphitheatre. Wesley made Gwennap one of his most frequent visits, identifying with the mining communities and their social prob-

St Newlyn East

lems and thirst for his form of religion. Gwennap Pit still has a special service every Whit Monday, and has had since John's death.

The development of Methodism was not always smooth. Wesley himself didn't see it as a breaking away from the established Church. In fact he deliberately arranged his meetings so as not to clash with those of the local Church. He expected the people to attend both!

At Trewint is a cottage where Wesley stayed many times as a guest of Digory and Elizabeth Isbell. These two lived up to Wesley's hope of continuing to worship in the local church. At Altarnun their epitaph on the tombstone of 1805, states, "The first who entertained the Methodist preachers in this county, and lived and died in that connection, but strictly adhered to the duties of the Established Church."

Gradually the Church was losing patience with the Methodists and open hostility forced a split. In 1745 the Vicar of St Hilary wrote, "We have only one Methodist in the Parish, an infamous woman of Marazion, fit only to associate with so infamous a sect."

The enthusiasm for the new ways of religion resulted in a mushrooming of little chapels all over Cornwall, built and financed by local people. There also came a new breed of preachers who had to be trained. These little chapels were plain and simple, a reflection of the basis of early Methodism in the county. One preacher who stood out for his industry and dedication was Billy Bray (q.v.).

John and more so Charles, wrote many of the hymns that became loved and a very important part of the services. Unpaid 'local preachers' spoke fervently with the plain language of their daily lives. They varied from the upbeat of an optimist to those who preached fire and damnation. Above all Methodism was lively and about a good and Christian life. It developed at a time when the established Church was in a self-satisfied deep sleep.

MEVAGISSEY

Its name sounds puzzling but is in fact a combination of the names of two saints to whom the church is dedicated, Meva and Issey.

Why not visit this charming fishing village in the autumn or winter? There will be a lot less people milling about and you will be able to see and appreciate the boats, smell the sea and not the chips, and what's more park!

Under the summer plumage of visitor-fodder, just like many other Cornish fishing villages, there is a genuine and active place central to the South Cornish coast. Historically the fishing here was varied employing up to 300 men as well as all of the ancillary workers needed to prepare and pack the fish for markets near and far. Like many other fishing harbours the migrating pilchards were an annual bonanza. In later years Mevagissey was one of the pioneers in pilchard canning. The harbour's piers are quite old, but a major advancement occurred with the outer harbour adding extra shelter from 1890. The former lifeboat house is still here but has had no boat since the 1930's.

Two sons of Mevagissey are worthy of note. The first, born c.1770, was Andrew Pears, the son of a local farmer who went to London to seek his fortune. In 1789 he produced and sold his first transparent soap bars.

Jonathon Barron was a snooker master of the 1960's and 70's. He became English Amateur Champion and later the World Champion. He scored the first live televised century break in a pro-am tournament and undoubtedly would have been a top 16 professional today.

Meva welcomes the visitors and their trade, but in a detached sort of way. Mevagissey men are a proud and fiercely independent breed.

MINACK THEATRE

Dramatically perched halfway down the cliff at Porthcurnow in Cornwall's far west is the famous open-air theatre of Minack. Painstakingly and lovingly developed over time by Miss Rowena Cade, it is cut into the granite and enhanced with man-made balustrades and walls. Row upon row of tiered seating made comfortable with cushions support a blanket-wrapped audience in awe of a situation of great beauty and atmosphere. There are no curtains or backdrops save that of the sea. Weather permitting, the Minack experience is not to be missed.

MINING

Although the collecting of minerals in Cornwall goes back more than 2,000 years, the early extraction was from alluvial deposits found in gravels and sand in streams and mud deposits. The first miners, working underground, were probably from the 15th century, at a time when the easy surface deposits were all but exhausted. They learned to follow the veins of ore from cliffs and riverbanks forming tunnels and so creating mining.

Although tin was the first metal in Cornwall to be mined in any quantity, 300 years ago attention turned to copper, thereby increas-

ing the number of miners needed for the new extraction. Mines needed to go deeper but natural drainage to the water table made this very difficult. To the rescue came the steam engine driven pump, first by Watt in 1777, and then much improved by Trevithick.(q.v.) The Cornish pump became used in mines all over the world.

By the mid 19th century Cornish mines were producing three-quarters of the world's copper and about half of the tin. Hundreds of mines with miles of tunnels, some going out under the sea, were each at full capacity.

The miner worked to an unusual employment system. Instead of a wage, a contract was agreed whereby the miner received a percentage of the value of the ore, a system known as 'tribute'. To do well the miner had to have a good knowledge and experience of ore quality and be prepared to gamble. The general labour of shaft digging and the creation of vents or adits was less well paid and known as 'tutwork'.

Mining was hard work and generally unhealthy. Walking to work and then using ladders to descend and at the end of the day to ascend many hundreds of fathoms from different levels was the unhealthy norm. Temperatures where they laboured were high, 115 degrees in the United Mines of St Day, and the air of poor quality. Statistics of c.1850 show that the average age

of death of a miner was only 47! Miners often worked as a pair or three with one turning the drill as the other or others beat with heavy hammers producing deep holes for blasting. Their only light was from candles fixed to the hat with a dab of clay. Although some boys would go underground at ten years, women and girls, bal maidens, only worked at the surface.

Modernisation gradually took place with lift cages to transport the miners and better ventilation systems. However a severe decline in Cornish mining was to come. During the early 1870's deposits of cheap to work tin and copper were found in other parts of the world, leading to little demand for our ores. Mines closed all over the county leaving just a few, mainly in Redruth, Camborne and down West to soldier on.

In recent decades we have seen the demise of such mines as Geevor, Wheal Jane, Mount Wellington and South Crofty. Of the future, it all depends on the demands set by world market prices. South Crofty believes it can again be profitable with improved techniques and mining other ores in addition to tin. In Cornwall's past, as well as ores of tin and copper, lead, zinc, iron and tungsten were also extracted.

Is there a future for Cornish mining? Never say never!

MOUSEHOLE

Named from a large cave in the cliff nearby, Mousehole is usually pronounced Mowzel. The name Porthenys was sometimes used, meaning the harbour or cove of the island, referring to St Clement Isle at the entrance.

One of Cornwall's most picturesque little harbours, one based on a fishing industry then more important than Newlyn. It is impossible to miss and not be impressed by the massive granite rocks that form one of the ancient piers. The village is a cluster of narrow streets with little cottages, be sure not to try to drive through! Look out for Mousehole's oldest buildings. One of these is the former inn 'The Keigwin Arms. This and one other, 'The Standard', were the only buildings to survive the Spanish invasion of 1595. Raids were also carried out at Paul, Newlyn and Penzance.

Each year on 23th December, Mousehole celebrates Tom Bawcock's Eve. The story, of which there is more than one version, is set sometime in the past when, following many days of stormy weather, the village had all but run out of food. Brave widower, Tom Bawcock risked his life to go to sea to fish. He returned with seven species of fish including pilchards, which were made into stargazey pie to feed the people. The fish pie is so named because some

whole fish are poked through the pastry crust 'gazing starward'! The pies are still made at the Ship Inn.

The village has always supplied brave men to man the Penlee Lifeboat. None will ever forget the disaster of 1981, an account of which may be found in the section 'Lifeboats'.

MURDOCH, WILLIAM

In 1784 Murdoch* had made a model steam powered locomotive which he tested near Redruth Parish Church, much to the fright of passing ladies, this a few years before Trevithick.(q.v.) William Murdoch, a Scotsman, had come to Cornwall as an engineer to erect

and maintain first the Newcomen and then the Watt engines being used in the mines. In 1792, then working as Boulton's agent, Murdoch experimented with coal gas lighting. He 'cooked' coal in a closed vessel and piped the gas to jets arranged around his home in Redruth's Cross Street for a light superior to candles or oil. In 1802 he fitted plant to gaslight part of Boulton's Soho Foundry in Birmingham. In the following year he lit the whole works using the improved bat's wing jets.

He experimented with compressed air, developing the pneumatic message system used by Harrod's. He also perfected the sun and planet gearing system.

Each year Redruth celebrates his life with a special Murdoch Day.
*Murdock would seem to be the spelling he used in later days.

N

NATIONAL TRUST

The National Trust has a large holding of both land and property in Cornwall. As would be expected, with a long coastline of contrasting grandeur and beauty, much has been donated or purchased over the Trust's hundred odd years. From Morwenstow to the Land's End, the Lizard and back to the Tamar, over 120 miles are Trust protected. This includes such places as Bedruthan, Pentire, St Agnes Beacon, Godrevy, Gurnard's Head, Treryn Dinas, St Michael's Mount, Loe Bar, Mullion Cove, Kynance, Lizard Point, St Anthony Head, Nare Head, Dodman Point and Gribben Head.

Properties include:

Anthony House in S.E. Cornwall which was a location for the filming of the 2010 Alice in Wonderland.

On the banks of the Tamar is Cotehele, the former home of the Edgcumbe family. Building began around 1480 and continued for 150 years. The restored sailing barge *Shamrock* berths at the quay.

Trerice, near Newquay, is a delightful Elizabethan manor house of 1571.

Lanhydrock, near Bodmin, is by the River Fowey and was the home of the Robartes family.

St Michael's Mount (q.v.), opposite Marazion, was originally the site of a Benedictine Chapel established by Edward the Confessor. The castle is 14th century.

Pool, between Redruth and Camborne has two preserved beam engines that were used in the mines.

For Trelissick, Trengwainton and Glendurgan, see 'Gardens of Cornwall'.

NEWLYN

The origin of the name is not from the English 'new', but originally was Lulyn which Padel suggests probably means pool for a fleet of boats.

Now one of the country's leading fishing ports, Newlyn can well average over 100 commercial fishing vessels using its facilities. During the second half of the 19th century extensive quay work was carried out enabling the port to function at all states of the tide and in all weathers. It was soon to establish itself as a major force in the fishing industry. Drift netting was well in advance of its competitors with Newlyn soon becoming the chief mackerel port.

Times were not always easy however. The steam drifters from the East Coast ports barged their way into the fishery with no respect for the Cornish practice of not fishing on a Sunday. The markets were flooded on a Monday with the local boats getting lower prices on the following days. The Mount's Bay men took action in 1896 boarding the East Coast boats and dumping their catches. They chained the harbour entrance and got similar support from neighbouring Porthleven and Mousehole. The effect of the Newlyn riots however was to some degree nullified by immediate neighbour Penzance letting the visitors in! The ill feeling generated never totally healed.

For many years road stone from Penlee Quarry was shipped from here, while in 1915 the Ordnance Survey tidal observatory was established to continually monitor tidal data.

Newlyn is now a leading fishing port with a turnover of more than £18,000,000 per year (2004). Beam trawlers, conventional trawlers, gill-netters and inshore boats all work from here. Recent years has seen a resurgence of the pilchard fishery (q.v.) with the fish being marketed as Cornish sardines.

Leader of the Chartist Movement, William Lovett, was born in Newlyn in 1800. He led the movement towards political change through pressure and non-violence to improve the lot of the working man. He formed the National Union of Working Classes and had proposals to improve their education.

Newlyn Harbour

76

NEWLYN SCHOOL

Stanhope Forbes and his fellow artists were regarded as revolutionaries of their time – the 1880's and 90's. These 'plein air' painters captured the Cornwall that they saw with their own eyes. They were attracted to Newlyn, (others to St Ives) and formed one of the great movements in British art. The binding ethic of the Newlyn School was the belief that it was essential to paint in the reality of the open air. Artists sitting on harbour walls behind easels was something new and reminiscent of the continent. Fisher folk and fishing boats were the most popular subjects by such artists as: Stanhope Forbes, Walter Langley, Ralph Todd, Frank Bramley, Lamorna Birch and Alfred Munnings.

The painting that established Newlyn as an artists' colony was Stanhope Forbes' A Fish Sale on a Cornish Beach shown at the Royal Academy in 1885. A study of white sky, suffused daylight, quiet dull sea, many reflections and fish on the sand – all carefully arranged.

NEWQUAY

There is something unimaginative about the word 'new' when used to name a place. Why Newtown (Newton) or The New Inn? Was there no one with a bit of creativity? It becomes a bit silly when no longer new. The name Newquay dates from about 1440 when the construction of a quay is mentioned. The new structure was built on the shore of Towan Blistra, the first element of which is sand dunes. What a pity that the name was overlooked.

"Newquay is in Cornwall without being Cornish, and is one of the few towns which has no 'saint' belonging to it. Most of the towns in the peninsula date back to the days of saints and giants, and then crystallize somehow. Newquay didn't grow up that way, and was content to remain until quite recently the habitation of a score of fisher families, who lived by beach-combing and pilchard seining. If the town of today (1906) were wiped out, there would remain the old fish-cellars, a few weather-beaten cottages, and the Huer's Hut on the Headland." Succinctly put by J Henry Harris in his Cornish Saints and Sinners.

Newquay's transition from fishing village to holiday resort didn't happen without some friction. When building work for a huge hotel on the 'public' Headland, where fishermen dried their nets, was started, riots occurred to halt progress. The Headland Hotel did however eventually win the day. Murray in his Handbook for Devon and Cornwall, 1859, says that "Newquay is a small but rising watering-place, where the pilchard fishery is pursued on a considerable scale." and he adds, "Newquay is to be the terminus of a railway... it will run from Par." The train was to bring visitors to the town by the thousand, especially com-

The Newquay Huers Hut

ing from the industrial centres of the country.

Blessed with wonderful beaches and coastal scenery Newquay could not go wrong. Expansion took place at a frightening speed. Firstly hotel-staying visitors, then the B&B bucket and spaders, together with the caravanners and campers and the self-caterers, they all crammed in. Where could Newquay go from there? Well it still holds on to the family resort label, but is under pressure. The last few years, fuelled by longer opening hours and a higher disposable income in the young, together with a freer youth lifestyle, have brought problems. Bad publicity spread across the popular press and the television news has placed a black mark on the town. Efforts are being made to put things right, but it may take some time.

Newquay is the surf capital of Britain with Fistral Beach to the fore. It holds many competitive events, attracting the World's best, establishing a surf culture which brings valuable income to the town.

Let Folliott-Stokes, visiting Cornwall in 1928, have the final words. "Nature has been very kind to Newquay. She has given her, amongst other gifts, a headland that protrudes far out into the Atlantic, and several miles of hard, broad sands, bordered by cliffs honeycombed with caves, which offer bathing facilities probably unequalled in the Kingdom."

NEWQUAY AIRPORT

A civilian airfield to the east of Newquay was set up in 1933, but from the demands of Word War II for airfields in many county locations saw it become R.A.F. St Mawgan by 1943. The runways can take very fast and very large aircraft, Concorde has landed there, thanks to the investment of the United States Air Force occupation for the strategic bomber base set up during the 'Cold War'. Just a few years ago the Americans left the base with it reverting to the R.A.F. Their final squadron to be based there was RAF 203R, a Sea King helicopter unit.

Eventually, with the military having no immediate use for St Mawgan, it became the civilian Newquay Airport in December 2008. Services link with many British airports as well as some flights to Western Europe.

O

OPIE, JOHN

John Opie was from Mithian. The son of a St Agnes miner, he made his way to London in 1782. Great interest for this artist was shown by Joshua Reynolds who appreciated Opie's portraiture. For a time he was very successful becoming Professor of Painting to the Royal Academy. Six of his lectures are still accepted as relevant today being written with a literary skill. Opie later retired to Cornwall where he painted many well known people.

OYSTER FISHERY

This ancient and sustainable fishery is mainly based in the Fal and Helford estuaries with smaller production in the Camel, Fowey and Percuil areas. The majestic, classic, gaff cutter working boats dredge the more open sections of the estuaries, some of these vessels being of considerable age.

Carew in his Survey of Cornwall, 1606, writes of the oyster dredges, "A thick strong, net fastened to three spills of iron and drawn at the boat's stem, gathering whatever it meeteth lying in the bottom of the water, out of which, when it is taken up, they cull oysters and cast away the residue, which they term gard, and serveth as a bed for the oysters to breed in."

Where the estuary narrows, small rowing boats tow and winch a dredge to 'fish' the creeks. The dredges used have changed little over the years being about a metre wide shaped like a net bag with iron bars at the opening. Any oyster that will pass through ring of 68 mm. diameter must he put hack to grow on. After harvesting, only allowed, from October to March, the oysters are purified before selling. Many are exported but, the Falmouth Oyster Festival up to 10,000 are reported to be consumed!

Both native and Pacific oysters are farmed at The Duchy Oyster Farm on the Helford involving some five million a year. The future for this Cornish industry is dependent upon many factors including the willingness of the skilled fishermen to continue the historic practices and the continual threat from disease, the slipper limpet and chemical contamination.

P

PADSTOW

The only real shelter on the North Coast between St Ives and Bideford, Padstow is guarded by the notorious Doom Bar – a constantly shifting sand bank, horrendous in bad weather. Padstow nestles in a hollow looking out to the broad expanse of the Camel estuary.

A town of great antiquity, once known as Lodeneck, and later Petrockstow, it had a considerable trade in timber, was an embarkation point for Ireland and has always traded in fish. Until the 1960's it was the terminus of the Southern Railway. The track bed is now the very popular Camel Trail for walkers and cyclists. Padstow is now very much a holiday resort with much recent publicity generated by chef Rick Stein with his restaurant and television coverage.

Across the estuary is Rock, an up-market holiday retreat served by a passenger ferry from Padstow. Rock has the well known Sharp's Brewery, one of its ales being 'Doom Bar'.

May Day in the town is legendary with the celebrating of each new summer. At midnight people leave the pubs and prepare to sing the Morning Song, which begins:

Unite and unite, and let us all unite,
For summer is a coming today,
And bright is your bride that lies by your side,
In the merry morning of May.

At least 17 verses have been recorded! Soon after 8.00 a.m. the people assemble again to prepare the ancient hobby-horses for their annual excursion into the streets. One, mainly black with a wide hooped skirt, little can be seen of the man underneath. At 10.00 a.m. the horse (oss) leaves the Golden Lion accompanied by a gang highly dressed and with some musical instruments. At present there are two osses, blue and red, each with followers wearing their preferred colours. The words of the Morning Song are once again heard. After a time a new song is heard:

Oh where is St.George?
Oh where is he, O?
He's out in his long boat,
all on the salt sea, O.

What the Obby Oss celebration means to Padstow people is clearly stated in this excerpt from the Padstonian Souvenir Programme of 1996. The Red Oss writes,

"The bones of every Padstow Boy are fired by the Hobby-horse. As soon as a child is able to lisp its parents' names it will chant the glorious strains of our ancient Festival Song and will usher in May's first merry morn . . . And shall we allow aliens and strangers to usurp our pleasures, and rob us of our birth right, that we have inherited from Mother to Daughter, from Father to Son? No we will not! 'Cala Me Bys Vyken!'" (May Day for ever!)

PAR

A puzzling name which both Dexter (Cornish Names, 1926) and Padel (Cornish Place-Names, 1988) agree that it developed from the shortening of 'porth', a small bay.

Par is a port dominated by and almost entirely for china clay. Entrepreneur Treffry was the developer, needing an outlet for his copper ore that was nearer to Lanescot than the established port of Fowey. From the 1820's he undertook the massive development of breakwaters and piers to create an impressive port. Treffry established other facilities including a smelting works, brickworks, ship building, a pilchard fishery and much more. He built a rail and leat viaduct (aqueduct) to link his clay pits to his port.. This, to be found in the Luxulyan valley, is well worth a visit.

Par can now take ships of up to 2,300 tonnes and up to 19 at a time. Larger ships use Fowey, now the main clay exporter.

PASCOE, LIEUTENANT JOHN

John Pascoe, sometimes spelt Pasco, was born near Torpoint in 1774 and is remembered for his contribution to Nelson's famous flag signal at Trafalgar in 1805. In his role as Signal Officer he was to hoist the famous signal 'England expects that every man will do his duty'. Pascoe suggested 'expects' be substituted for 'confides' since the former was in the signal book, whereas 'confides' would have to be spelled out letter by letter. Nelson quickly agreed. Pascoe recorded, "His Lordship came to me and after ordering certain signals to be made, he said, 'Mr Pascoe, I wish to say to the fleet – England confides that every man will do his duty.' and he added, 'You must be quick . . .' I replied, 'If Your Lordship will permit me to substitute the confides for expects, the signal will soon be completed because the word expects is in the vocabulary and confides must be spelt.' His Lordship replied, in haste, and with seeming satisfaction, 'That will do, Pascoe, make it directly'."

Pascoe was eventually promoted to Admiral of the Red in 1852.

PASSMORE EDWARDS, JOHN – (1823 - 1911)

His name rings a bell doesn't it? But why? You have probably seen it on your local library building.

Passmore Edwards was born in Blackwater. the son of a carpenter, who would become a journalist, a newspaper owner and a philanthropist. He became the editor of a leading London newspaper, *The Echo*, which he was able to buy in 1876. He became the Liberal M.P. for Salisbury but soon became disgruntled with politics. Twice refusing a knighthood, he became unpopular because of his opposition to the Boer War.

A champion of the working classes he is remembered as a generous benefactor. Within the space of 14 years, 70 major buildings were established with his bequests. These include hospitals, libraries, schools, convalescence homes and art galleries. He gave much to the Workers' Educational Association (W.E.A.)

In Cornwall he financed public libraries at Bodmin, Camborne, Falmouth, Launceston, Liskeard, Penzance, St Ives and Truro.

PASTY

Don't call it a Cornish pasty,* there is no other! All of us Cornish know how a proper pasty is made. We were heavily influenced by those of our mothers' or grandmothers' making, naturally looking upon their creations as archetypal.

In modern times most use beef skirt, potato (sliced not diced), onion and turnip – that's what the Cornish call swede, seasoned, a knob of butter, in a short-crust pastry jacket, crimped at the side and baked for about an hour. Note that all the ingredients must be raw. Any divergence from this classic recipe must be treated with caution.

It wasn't always like this however. It is only in the last 100 to 150 years that the general populace regularly consumed beef. Mutton, pork or rabbit were sometimes available, but at times the pasty only contained vegetables. Coastal areas would also have used fish as a filling. The idea that fruit was put at one end to provide a built in dessert was probably not common but may have been evident in season.

The pasty was designed to be carried and eaten from hand. Traditionally the croust (lunch) of the miner, it was taken in a cloth or cloth bag to be consumed as a midday meal. The pastry, of course, had to be robust and 'stand up' to its surroundings. A story is told of a man recently married to a cook who had formerly been in the service of a wealthy family. He went to work at the mine one day with a pasty of his wife's making. On his return he was asked "How did you like your pasty?"

"Aw, a wad'n no good at all," came the disappointed reply, "Time I got down fifty fathoms a were scat to lembs (broken into pieces). The wans mother made wad'n break if they faaled to the bottom of the shaft. They were pasties, you!"

For some reason misunderstandings have become more common in recent years as to the way the pasty was held. No! The crimp is not a handle allowing dirty hands to avoid the main body of the pasty leading to it (the crimp) being discarded at the end of the meal. What nonsense. Any miner labouring intensely for hours would not throw away precious fuel, apart possibly with one exception. A pasty is eaten from one end to the other, and often out of a bag. Some deviations from the norm are acceptable, my mother would often make one extra pasty on pasty day, to be eaten sliced and cold for tea. Left over pasty is often fried and extra ingredients like egg or parsley are to some people's taste. As for the exception, the superstitious miner might leave just a few crumbs for the Knockers!

The term 'teddy oggy' is often heard for a pasty. It may be a potato-filled 'hogen' or 'whyogen' which was a Cornish word for a meal in a pastry case.

* 2011 has given European protection to the term 'Cornish' to be used only for pasties made in the County.

PAYNE, ANTHONY
'The Cornish Giant'

During the Civil War, in May 1643, a battle took place at Stratton in which the King's troops led by Sir Bevil Grenville of Stowe were victorious. One of those who took part was the Cornish 'giant' Anthony Payne. He stood 7 feet 2 inches tall and was broadly built with immense strength.

It was said that one Christmas Eve a boy was sent out from the Grenville household, taking with him a donkey, to fetch firewood. When he failed to return, Anthony Payne went in search. On finding him, Payne put both the boy and the donkey onto his shoulders and carried them home.

King Charles II, in thanks for Payne's loyalty during the War, commanded that his portrait be painted by the Court Artist, Sir Geoffrey Kneller. In it Payne, the Yeoman of the Guns, stands with his left hand holding a halberd (a spear and battle-axe combination) and his right on a cannon. This very large painting can be seen in the County Museum at Truro.

PENDENNIS & ST MAWES CASTLES

Two of a chain erected on the orders of King Henry VIII from 1538 under the threat of a French invasion.

Pendennis was completed in 1546 with St Mawes slightly earli-

Pendennis Castle

er in 1543. Below Pendennis, on the rocks, was a Tudor blockhouse, dismantled in 1654, the one at St Mawes still remains.

During the Civil War the Royalists were under severe pressure, and at Tresillian Bridge, near Truro, the strugglers were defeated by Fairfax and his Parliamentary army which had swept through the west. This is where Pendennis Castle comes into the story. In 1643 a Cornishman, Colonel John Arundell was appointed Governor there. On the 17th March 1646 Fairfax took up his position at nearby Arwenack and demanded the surrender of the Castle. Arundell replied that he was seventy years old and could not have many years to live, and therefore would not in his old years blemish his honour. A siege continued for five months until there was no food left, even the horses had been consumed! The surrender was honourable with the ragged band marching out to a drum accompaniment. With the exception of Raglan Castle, Pendennis was the last stronghold that held out for the King. St Mawes Castle, being virtually impossible to defend from the landward side, was surrendered by its Governor Hannibal Bonython earlier in March 1646.

Both castles are designed on a circular theme using polygons with a strong sense of symmetry. Each has a drawbridge and portcullis.

PENHALIGON, DAVID

The much loved and fondly remembered Liberal M.P. for Truro and St Austell had his life cut short on 19th December 1983 in a car crash on ice at Truck Fork, Probus. David was a Truro boy, educated at Truro School and later an apprentice engineer with Holman's at Camborne. He is remembered for his humour and Cornish pride soon becoming a favourite at Westminster. He championed the mining and fishing industries and even advocated a National Minimum Wage. Without doubt he would have become Liberal Party Leader.

His Cornish roots were to the fore when asking in the House about train services. Hansard reports him as saying, "The Honourable Member for the South Hams (Stein) will know that the Cornish have a fairly flexible attitude to time. I was brought up with a marvellous word called 'd'rectly', it will arrive 'd'rectly'. Anything that will arrive 'd'rectly' may arrive next minute or in half an hour."

PENRYN

A proud and proper small Cornish town – The Borough. Its enfranchisement to borough status goes back to 1236. Some years later the Collegiate Church of Glasney was founded on the river shore, built with stone from Caen, in France. Its purpose was to promote the Church's influence in the far west of the Exeter Diocese, following the demise of the monasteries and the creation of the Church of England. Glasney was dissolved in 1548.

In the 18th century Penryn was a thriving port and commercial centre. Cargoes handled included coal, tin ore, fish and dressed granite. The granite was exported to many countries and especially to London where it was used for the London Bridge.

Poet Laureate, Robert Southey, didn't think much of the town when he commented on a coach journey from Falmouth up country in 1802. "Penryn, whose ill-built and narrow streets seem to have been contrived to make as many acute angles in the road, and take the traveller up and down as many steep declivities as possible in a given direction." He would have been impressed with Penryn's make-over of 1975, the Housing Action Plan. Many old cottages were updated and made sound, all in a much lauded project.

To many of its neighbours, Penryn is 'Shag Town'. One likely explanation is related by Rodney Newman (Captain Pete) of Tolverne in his 1950's little book, The Charm of the Fal. "Cattle were regularly shipped from Spain to Penryn. After a long voyage and under appalling conditions they were quickly unloaded and disposed of, the sick and the dying slaughtered on the spot with their offals dumped in the river. The shag, a black seabird slightly smaller than a cormorant used to congregate in their thousands on the river banks, waiting for the boats' arrival, as gulls do today with fishing boats, for a meal."

Penryn is now a University Town (q.v.) with the campus at Tremough.

PENTEWAN

If you can ignore the caravan park which dominates this St Austell Bay resort you will find a most interesting site of industrial archaeology in Pentewan village. The sea has forsaken the little harbour which was started in 1818 and financed by the Hawkins family to ship china clay and offer an alternative to Charlestown. Pentewan had been a place for the shipping of the much prized 'Pentewan Stone' in great demand for prestigious buildings.

China clay was the reason for the port's development, in 1831 it handled one third of the county's clay, but ironically was the main reason for its demise. The continual discharge of the 'white' rivers and streams of the St Austell area caused sand-bars and choking silt deposits which could not be controlled. Even the construction of holding ponds to flush the channels proved ineffective.

Clay was brought to the port by a light railway of 2ft. 6ins. gauge which ran down the valley from St Austell from 1829. It closed in 1919.

Liz Luck in her South Cornish Harbours, 1988, sums up Pentewan's industrial ghosts. "There is something tragic about its landlocked dock basin bearded with reeds, ducks dappling the water, the cottages grouped about . . . the empty harbour. There is an air of expectancy . . . the old dock gates seem poised to open, the capstans ready to turn . . . The dock is stranded, separated from the sea by 400 yards of land."

PENTREATH, DOLLY

Dolly grew up in a Cornish speaking family and folklore has made her out to be the last natural speaker of the language. If so, were her final years spent in lonely monologue?

Drew, in his History of Cornwall (1780), quoting Barrington who was investigating spoken Cornish in 1768, writes, "She does indeed talk Cornish as readily as others do English, being bred up from a child to know no other language, nor would she (if we may believe her) talk a word of English before she was past 20 years of age." Barrington was taken to Mousehole to meet Dolly Pentreath in person, "I desired to be introduced as a person who had had a wager that there was not one who could converse in Cornish; upon which Dolly spoke in an angry tone for two or three minutes, and in a language which sounded very like Welsh."

In 1777, the year of Dolly's death, Barrington found another Cornishman, John Nancarrow of Marazion, aged 45, able to speak Cornish. Nancarrow said that, "In my youth I had learned the language from the country people, and could then hold a conversation in it."

The stone in Paul Churchyard wall, set up in 1860, contains two errors. It runs, "Here lieth interred Dorothy Pentreath who died in 1778." She doesn't lie where the stone is and she died in 1777 on December 26th.

It would seem naive to believe that any one person could have been the last to use a language when a lengthy intermixing of vocabularies would have naturally occurred. No person would give up the Cornish words for things in their life and suddenly adopt new ones, the beginnings of dialect were being formed. It is true that the spoken Cornish Language slowly died out on a course from East to West. It was also true that Dolly was a fish 'jouster' (hawker) of some character and therefore well known in her area. So let us say that Dolly Pentreath was of a generation that was the last to speak Cornish on a daily basis.

Let Thurstan Peter in his History of Cornwall for Schools, 1905, have the last words. "The legend of Dolly Penreath 'the last person who spoke Cornish' has been well said to justify the first words of her epitaph, 'Here lieth'."

PENZANCE

Penzance – the holy headland, probably from the 700 year old chapel of St Mary. Once, like Newlyn, it was the poor relation of Mousehole (q.v.) and even Marazion. It was kick-started by the harbour charter of 1512 and the borough status about 100 years later. In the mid 1660's it became a stannary town for the assaying of West Cornwall's tin.

Improvements to the harbour, including new piers and a dry-dock,

gradually took place. Trade was substantial with tin ore exports to the fore. The late 19th century saw further enhancement to the port facilities with a floating dock and a new dry-dock, later to be owned by Holman's, together with the Ross swing bridge.

Since 1858, Penzance has been the mainland arm of the steamer link to the Isles of Scilly. But with updates needed there is much controversy over alterations to the port facilities. The main argument concerns the balance between a modern handling and shipping facility and the history of the present pier at Battery Rocks. With the prospect of the town losing its helicopter link, things could get worse if some common ground cannot be found.

In the town Sir Humphry Davy (q.v.) looks down Market Jew Street with its high pavement. The unusually named Causeway Head is a pedestrianised street of interestingly varied shops. Running from the railway station to Newlyn, first passing the harbour, one soon gets to the broad expanse of the seafront complete with classic open-air swimming pool At times bleak, in can be bad news in a southerly gale.

Penzance's mixture of maritime and market town allows it to function as the capital of Penwith.

PERRANPORTH

Now an impressive and important surfing beach and holiday resort, but its history is of mining. At the eastern end of Perran Sands mines were dotted along the Great Perran Iron Lode, a source, not only of iron, but other minerals as well. At the western end along the cliffs, and around the area that is now the town, the mines were mainly for copper with some tin.

The long stretch of sand, backed for most of its length by a huge area of dunes is one of Cornwall's gems. Perran Sands has the remains, now buried for preservation, of St Piran's (q.v.) Oratory, probably the oldest remaining relic of Celtic Christianity in the country. Nearby is a sturdy granite Cornish Celtic Cross.

The western end of the beach is edged with cliffs, caves and natural arches, with the prominent Chapel Rock standing alone. The town itself is not graced with little streets or charming cottages, but is a relatively modern combination of hotels, guest-houses and terraces of domestic dwellings. In the 1920's it was described as "in a somewhat embryo condition."

Perranporth Sundial

An indication of Perranporth's very young tourist industry is in its total omission from Black's Guide to Cornwall of 1874, and with the 1919 edition having, "the little watering place of Perranporth has been much in favour with Truro's excursionists, and begins to come into wider notice as a haven of refuge from the 'madding crowd'."

The resort was served by the torturous rail link that ran from Chacewater and looped to Newquay. Amazingly Perranporth had two stations!

PHOENICIANS,
Who were they?

The Phoenicians keep cropping up in Cornwall's history. Everything from traders in metals to initiators of saffron cake (q.v.) and clotted cream (q.v.). Who were they?

Phoenicia was the name of the strip of land in the Eastern Mediterranean between the mountains of Lebanon and the sea, now Syria. It included the city of Tyre. The Phoenicians themselves dominated at the end of the second millennium B.C. They were certainly seafaring travellers and craftsmen who may have visited Scilly and Cornwall.

With the tin trade in mind, the respected historian A.K. Hamilton Jenkin says in The Cornish Miner, 1927, "that there was in all probability, a very ancient commerce of tin between some ports of South

West Britain and the Mediterranean." He continues to question the handing down of facts intermingled with fiction pointing out that there is no well documented history of the Cornish tin industry until the middle of the 12th century A.D. "It is only fair, however," he wrote, "to say that as the learned have had their theories, so the simple have evolved romances to fill the gaps where history itself is wanting. Among the latter the coming of the Phoenicians is still in full possession at this very day."

The Cassiterides, where it is reputed that the Phoenicians got their tin, is said by some to be the Scillies, but it could equally be elsewhere. The same reasoning can be used for Ictis being St Michael's Mount. Ictis is described by Diodorus Siculus and Plinny the Elder with some correlation in imagination to the Mount, but everything doesn't tie up. One thing that the Phoenicians did do, apparently, was to keep all their trading places a very close secret.

PILCHARD FISHERY

The great mainstay of the Cornish fishing trade for centuries up to the mid 19th was a fish smaller than a herring and larger than its juvenile stage the sardine, the pilchard. From the Atlantic it reached the Cornish coast in mid July, remaining in coastal waters until November or December. For nearly all of Cornwall's inhabitants the pilchard was the staple diet, eaten fresh in summer and salted down for winter. During August look-outs were posted on cliff vantage points after news of the pilchards' arrival in West Cornwall quickly spread. The look-out or 'huer', armed with a furze bush, or similar, would watch for a dark shadow on the sea, indicating to his experienced eye a shoal of pilchards. Meanwhile boats, nets and men would be waiting. The 'huer' would indicate, first by calling 'hevva' through a large megaphone trumpet, and then by a simple form of semaphore with the furze to the fishermen the direction in which the shoal was going. The word 'hevva' has the Cornish language meaning of shoalling fish. The boats were launched and the seine net was shot with the object being to entrap the whole shoal of hundreds of thousands of fish. Three boats made up a typical fishing village's seining company, the 'stop' boat rowed by six men and carrying a massive main net of up to 400 yards long, the following boat of similar size which carried the 'tuck' net, and lastly the 'lurker' from which the head of the seine directed operations. The shoal was encircled by the main seine net. Capstans on the boat were used to haul the net tightly together and nearer to the shore. The fish were then taken from within the seine net by repeated shootings of the smaller 'tuck' seine.

Back on shore the next procedure was to get the pilchards into carts or barrows to the salting houses where the women and children layered them in salt. This process, called baulking, meant building a wall of fish three feet high and two feet wide. For about thirty days the pilchards would remain in baulk. Apart from those for local consumption, the rest were washed and carefully packed into hogsheads, a barrel of about 50 gallons containing some 3,000 fish, layer upon layer, tails to the centre. When full, a lid called a buckler was placed on top with a weighted pole continually pressing the fish. More and more pilchards would be added until the barrel was full. The oil that ran out of the cask was gullied into a pot. This 'train oil' was used to fuel the 'pilchard chills' that lit the cottages.

There was little demand for pilchards in England, but in Spain, Italy and to a lesser extent the West Indies there was a need to satisfy the strict religious observance. Harris in his *Cornish Saints and Sinners*, 1906, somewhat cynically recounts, "that it showed a fine spirit to feed poor benighted Italians who crossed themselves, and pouch a hundred thousand sterling a year for the trouble. Pickled pilchards he looked on as a bond of union between the two countries. Pilchards feed bodies, the Pope's souls and the shekels come here. Long live the pilchard!

Here's to the health of the Pope!
May he live to repent,
And add just six months to his Lent,
And tell all his vassals from Rome to the Poles,
There's nothing like pilchards for saving their souls."

PILOT GIGS

The Cornwall and Scilly pilot gig is a six oared rowing boat, though some had an auxiliary sail, built from Cornish elm. The exact build standard is now 32 feet in length with a beam of 4 feet 10 inches.

Originally in general use, they were later to take pilots to incoming or passing vessels, often from the Atlantic. The first boat got the contract, therefore the need for speed was created. The gigs also came into their own as 'lifeboats' quickly going to aid stricken ships or fishing boats.

The Newquay gig, *Treffry*, built by William Peters of St Mawes in 1838, acts as the blueprint for all others. In recent years one of the more prolific gig builders has been the late Ralph Bird of Devoran. Newquay Rowing Club also has the historic gigs, *Dove* (1820) and *Newquay* (1812), probably the oldest rowing boat in the world.

Today the gigs are involved in competition with well over 100 being used, not only, but mainly in Cornwall and the Isles of Scilly. Each year the World Championships are held in the Isles, the start of a hectic racing season. Gig racing has become a very successful Cornish sport enjoyed by men and women of all ages with a great camaraderie.

PISKIES
AND OTHER FAIRIES

According to Hunt in his Popular Romances of the West of England, 1864, there are five varieties of the Cornish fairy family:

> The small people
> Spriggans
> Piskies
> Buccas or Knockers
> Browneys

The most important are the middle three. The Spriggans are somewhat like the Trolls of Scandinavian legend. They are found only in stony outcrops such as cairns and cromlechs. They are remarkably mischievous and thieving. If ever a house was robbed, a child stolen, cattle carried away or a building demolished, it was the Spriggans! Whatever commotion took place in air, earth or water it was all down to these spirits.

The Piskie, or Pisky, is the most mischievous of all, and very unsociable. His favourite fun is to entice people into bogs by tricks of light as if from a cottage window. No Pisky could harm you if your coat was inside out and many a traveller would adopt this ruse while out at night. However there must have been a merry branch, for 'to laugh like a Pisky' is a popular saying.

Many a farmer was plagued by their night-time activity of riding the horses or chasing the cows.

In the mines the Knockers, or Buccas, were the little people who would be heard using their picks at the remotest parts of the mineral lodes repeating the blows of the miner's pick with great precision. Generally, the Knockers worked on profitable lodes only, so kindly indicating to the trusting miners where they could make good. It was very important therefore that the Knockers were never upset or bad luck would befall. To keep in their good books a few crumbs of food might be left at croust time.

A well known story concerns miner Tom Trevorrow who was busily eating his fuggan (a sort of heavy cake) when he heard the singing of the Buccas:

Tom Trevorrow! Tom Trevorrow! Leave some of the fuggan for Bucca, Or bad luck to thee tomorrow!

But Tom ate the lot and then heard:

Tommy Trevorrow, Tommy Trevorrow! We'll send thee bad luck tomorrow, Thou old curmudgeon to eat all thy fuggan, And not leave a didjan for Bucca.

After Trevorrow suffered great misfortune! Some say that the Knockers or Buccas are the souls of long since gone Jewish miners who worked in the very early days of mining.

91

PLACE-NAMES

One of the problems with place-names is that they originated long before local spelling was standardized. The early map-makers and scribes often wrote the names as they thought best without knowledge of their original make up. Some place-names have origins that are obvious, or at least not too difficult to explain, but some even leave experts to use the words 'possibly' or 'probably'.

As a starting point the oldest forms of a place-name give the best clues as to origin. Let us take the name Helston as an example. There would be no argument about the suffix 'ton' as English for farm, court of a manor or estate. But you could think that 'hels' comes from the Cornish 'heyl' (hayle), an estuary, leading to the plausible Heylston – estate on the estuary which Helston once was. History, however shows this not to be the case. Padel dates the following names for the town – Henlistone (1086), Hellestone (1187), and Helston (1365). From the first name we have Cornish 'hen' – old, and 'lys' – court, so Old Court of a Manor. In less than 300 years Henlistone had simplified to Helston.

Some Cornish place-names are self-explanatory being English in origin, for example, Blackwater, Charlestown and Newquay. Some villages may have grown up around an inn, Victoria, Bugle, Indian Queens and London Apprentice.

The saints make up a huge number of places, some appearing more than once throughout the county as does St Just. Some Cornish Language constructions follow:

Baldhu – *black mine*
Camborne (Cambron) – *crooked hill*
Egloshayle – *church on an estuary*
Hayle – *estuary*
Looe – *pool or inlet*
Penpol – *head of creek*
Penzance – *holy headland*
Poldhu – *Blackpool*
Polyphant (Todpool) – *toads' pool*
Porthtowan – *cove of dunes*
Portloe – *harbour inlet or pool*
Portscatho – *cove of boats*
Redruth – *ford that runs red*
Trenance – *farm in the valley*

For a comprehensive study see *Cornish Place-Names* by O.J. Padel, 1988.

PLAYING PLACES, PLEIN-AN-GWARRY

Cornish open-air theatres or 'rounds' were in the Language, plein-an-gwarry, places of the plays. There were many in the County, 'Rounds' as at St Just and Perranporth, and sites as at Plain an guare at Redruth and Playing Place near Truro are just some of them.

People enjoyed the 'Miracle Plays' performed at these places, some lasting for up to three days. With no formal seating the audiences were encouraged at times to dance to hold their interest and relieve their cramp. The 1504 dra-

Perran Round

ma, *The Life of Saint Meriasek* ends on a festive note:

Drink ye all with the play
We will beseech you
Before going hence
Pipers pipe ye at once!
We will, every son of the breast,

Go to dance,
Go ye or stay
Welcome shall ye be
Though ye be a week here.

During the play the actors took up fixed positions. God and Heaven was along the east and the Devil and Hell the north, while Saints and good people occupied the south. This left the audience in no doubt as to right and wrong!

The 16th century saw a decline in the production of Miracle Plays although visits from strolling players continued county-wide.

POETS OF THE PAST

Cornwall has inspired the poet in the same way that the writers of prose were inspired. Tennyson toured the county compiling a diary with such entries as *"glorious grass-green monsters of waves" and "with the long wave broke all down the thundering shores of Bude and Boss, then came a day as still as Heaven."*

A 29 year old Thomas Hardy, then an architect, spent time in Boscastle. Although remembered more as a novelist, he considered himself to be a poet. At St Juliot's Rectory in Boscastle he met and fell in love with Emma, the Rector's sister-in-law. The ensuing marriage was short lived but he continued to visit the county which gave him so much inspiration.

When I set out for Lyonesse,
A hundred miles away,
The rime was on the spray,
And starlight lit my lonesomeness,
A hundred miles away.

Two Cornish poets who were down to earth sons of mining and clay-working, were John Harris of Camborne and Jack Clemo of St Stephen. Harris worked as a miner in deep Dolcoath.

The heat, the cold, the sulphur
and the slime,
The grinding masses of the loos-
ened rock,
The scaling ladders, the incessant
grime
From the dark timbers and the
dripping block,
The lassitude, the mallet's fre-
quent knock,
The pain of thirst, when water
was so near,

The aching joints, the blasted
hole's rude shock,
Could not dash out the music
from his ear,
Or stay the sound of song which
ever burned clear.

Jack Clemo, never moving from his clay-land home, suffered blindness and deafness for most of his life.

My destiny is drawn
Sharp as the prongs
Of a clay tip against the dawn,
Unsoftened by the lark's song
Two gleaming fingers on the white
snout,
Grotesque above the clotted cone
Of carnal doubt,
They are Dogma's radiant bone.

A.L. Rowse, the historian specialising in the Elizabethan era, has written noteworthy verse as has Charles Causley of Launceston. The latter, much published and aiming at an all-age market, read his work with a delightful, soft, East Cornwall lilt. Of the sculptor Nevil Northy Burnard he wrote,

Here lived Burnard who with his
finger's bone
Broke syllables of light from the
moorstone,
Spat on the genesis of dust and
clay,
Rubbed with huge hands the blind-
ed eyes of day,
And through the seasons of the
talking sun
Walked, calm as God, the fields of
Altarnun.

A lover of Cornwall, and an accepted and adored poet, was John Betjeman. He spent many a holiday here as a child.

Where yonder villa hogs the sea
Was open cliff to you and me.
The many coloured caras fill
The salty marsh to Shilla Mill
And foreground to the hanging wood,
Are 'toilets' where the cattle stood.

These poets, despite their differences, all shared the atmosphere of their Cornwall. Today poetry writing is still very much to the fore.

POLPERRO

For the motorist the approach to Polperro is steep with a compulsory car park trap and promises nothing to the delight that is to come at the harbour. Crammed into a narrow cleft, it has cottages clinging to the valley sides. It manages to combine some fishing with a stifling number of visitors. John Betjeman rued the change in economic direction, "I can remember Polperro when it smelled of fresh fish instead of fried, and had one antique shop, a second-hand bookshop, a few artists' studios, and when fishing was still the main industry." Despite this view many boats still ply their trade, while there is no doubt that Polperro is on many holiday-maker's 'must visit' list.

PORTHLEVEN

On the eastern coast of Mount's Bay, Porthleven often receives the full force of the south-westerly gales. Its strong double harbour is often tested by nature while it protects a small fishing fleet. Pressure to build a harbour of refuge resulted from the many wrecks that had occurred in the area. The Loe Bar (q.v.), a short distance away, in particular had seen more than one tragedy. The loss of *HMS Anson* in 1807 with over 100 perishing, soon followed in 1810 by further wrecks and loss of life, led *The West Briton* of November 1810 to write of the latter, "had the harbour at Porthleven been completed these two vessels would have been saved."

The harbour was finally completed in 1825 and within a few years the mackerel and pilchard boats numbered over 60, together with an impressive drifter fleet. Ancillary industries to the maritime trade soon grew up, some of which supplied customers from a long

way away. "In the shed a fishing vessel is nearly complete. It is curious that the East-countrymen should come to this port for their boats, but some of them do, for Porthleven builders have the reputation of turning out the very best of work. Lying alongside the quay is a fishing yawl destined for Lowestoft . . . as taut and trim a craft as a man could wish to see. Bow like a steamer's, plenty of beam, about 40 tons register and fit to go round the world in." Folliott-Stokes, The Cornish Coast and Moor, 1928.

In 1853 the harbour was improved by new owners, Harvey's of Hayle, particularly in the creation of an inner harbour where boats could be kept afloat. For years tin and copper ores were exported from here.

Porthleven is still an impressive working harbour with interesting buildings around it. Dominating near the sea with its clock tower is a building given by Mr Bickford Smith of Trevarno to be an institute of learning. Despite an appreciated increase in the tourist trade, Porthleven remains an honest and hard working village.

PORTREATH

Pronounce it Por – treeth, it is Cornish porth treth, beach cove. Now a seaside resort with a fine beach, together with a small harbour with a few fishing craft, but at one time it was a busy, if not difficult, port.

Spurred by the need to export copper ore to Swansea, and to import coal for the mines of Camborne and Redruth, plans for a pier were first proposed in 1713. Francis Basset, an alternative name for Portreath was Basset's Cove, a landowner and mine adventurer was the driving force and motivator. By

1771 the coal requirements for Dolcoath Mine alone, for one month was the loads of 22 ships entering this difficult little harbour. Improvements were desperately needed and Francis Basset's son, Lord de Dunstanville, took complete control, repairing and expanding the facilities. It was then leased to the Foxes of Falmouth together with the Williams's of Scorrier to serve their vast mining interests.

To get the goods to and from Portreath mule trains were used, later to be replaced by horse-drawn wagons on a plateway in 1819, continuing until 1866. This ran from the harbour to North Downs Mine, through Scorrier to Poldice Mine with a branch to Treskerby. On the west of the valley is the derelict railway incline. This carried a mineral branch of the Hayle Railway running from Redruth. A stationary engine at the top of the parallel tracked incline hauled up the wagons with some help from the downgoing empties.

The harbour continued to be improved and remained in use for incoming coal into the 1960's.

Q

QUOITS

Quoits, cromlechs or dolmens are tombs where the dead were laid in a stone chamber rounded over with earth to form a barrow. They date from between 2,000 B.C. and 1,500 B.C. and therefore are some 3,500 to 4,000 tears old. There are nine in the county in varying stages of disrepair. Quoits consist of upright stones with a large capstone lying horizontally on the top. It must have been a Herculean task to move such heavy rocks probably using inclined slopes, hide ropes and a great deal of manpower!

Trethevy Quoit at St Cleer is well preserved with a sloping capstone and a double chamber. If you visit the site you could combine it with seeing the natural granite structure called The Cheesewring.

Zennor Quoit, also double chambered, is very large but unfortunately the capstone has fallen, probably due to a support being taken for other purposes. This has been a common problem for many archaeological remains which were seen as easy pickings by local builders and farmers.

Lanyon Quoit is one of the most impressive, and is easily found off the Penzance to Morvah road. Three uprights carry the massive capstone. It is reputed that a man on horseback could once have ridden under it!

A visit to the smaller Chun Quoit could easily be combined with seeing Chun Castle, built c.250 B.C. Other Cornish quoits include West Lanyon, Mulfra, Lanivet and Pawton (St Breock).

An ancient monument in West Penwith that creates much interest is the Men-an-tol, the holed stone. This has two standing stones and a rounded stone on edge with a 20 inch hole cut in the centre. Local folklore has it as the 'Crickstone' – those with bad backs or rickets would be cured by passing through it! Some believe that it is the remains of a quoit.

Lanyon Quoit

97

R

RAILWAYS

Cornwall's first true railway was the Redruth and Chasewater of 1826, constructed to take mineral ores from the area east of Redruth to Devoran and Point for shipment. Despite its name it never went to Chacewater! A narrow gauge china clay line was soon to follow in 1829 running from the St. Austell clay area to the little harbour of Pentewan. (q.v.) The Bodmin and Wadebridge Railway was started in 1834, three years before the first mainline railway elsewhere. It used standard gauge, steam power, and for the first time carried passengers.

The first train to cross the Tamar into Cornwall on Brunel's Royal Albert Bridge was in 1859. Using his favoured broad gauge allowed stability at high speeds. For a while there had to be changes at Truro because the West Cornwall Railway used standard gauge, but by 1866 the newly formed Cornwall Railway took the broad gauge to Penzance In 1892 an amazing weekend saw the whole line west of Exeter transformed to the standard gauge as it is today.

The first through coaches between Paddington and Penzance were run in 1867 with a journey time of 12 hours. By 1904 *The Cornish Riviera Express* (The Limited) managed the trip in only 7 hours!

The Great Western Railway's rival, The Southern Railway's route, known as the 'withered arm', served North Cornwall. Originating at Waterloo, it served Bodmin and Padstow among others.

Steam power ended in 1964 after a hundred years or so, to be replaced by diesel hydraulic and later diesel electric locomotion. At about the same time some of Cornwall's branch lines were closed. The Chacewater to Newquay and the Gwinear Road to Helston branches were gone. Mr Beeching's Act soon added Bude, Padstow and Fowey to the list. Luckily we still have branches to Falmouth, St Ives, Newquay (from Par), Looe and Gunnislake to enjoy.

REDRUTH

The red ford, rhyd – ford and ruth – red. Redruth is almost certainly named from the small stream running red with iron minerals, rather like the Red River a couple of miles to the west.

A town built up around mining, being in an area of extensive mineralization, Redruth's foundation was based on graft and mining prowess developed over many years. It was a town where miners lived, shopped and spent their leisure hours, as well as a place where mining business was transacted. So it was hardly a visitor attraction as Black's Guide to Cornwall of 1874 fears not to state, "a busy but dirty town, of one long street stretching out minor branches on every side, and flinging its arms, in the shape of dusty highways, into the quarries and mines which cover the surrounding district."

The decline in mining in the second half of the 19th century saw the town decimated by emigration, never again to be so prosperous. However the people are very proud of their town supporting its rugby team

fervently, not least when the 'Squareheads' of Camborne come to do battle on Boxing Day – the season of goodwill? – with the 'Choppers' of Redruth.*

Overlooking both towns is the imposing granite hill of Carn Brea, 750 feet above sea level. Historically it is a very important archaeological site, with an Iron Age hill fort and many other remains of significance. The 60 feet high granite monument is dedicated to Lord de Dunstanville (Basset), built by the miners of the district "to perpetuate the memory of a worthy man." The 'castle' was erected as a hunting lodge for the Basset family.

Every year Murdoch Day (q.v.) is celebrated in the town as is the famous Redruth Whitsun Fair.

* A butcher in the market was said to have chased a thief giving him 'three chops in the heel'.

RENEWABLE ENERGY

The use of renewable energy goes back a long way. The energy of moving water has been harnessed by man in two main ways. He used streams to power water-wheels both for machinery and for corn mills. A run of mills could take the energy of a single stream and recycle it over and over again. The simple wheel was later adapted to more efficient turbines, and in all but drought conditions, power was freely available.

Cornwall had many tide mills, especially on the Tamar and Fal estuaries, but also at Bude, Hayle, Padstow and St Minver. Nineteen have been traced within the county dating from the 15th century with all but two still working in the 19th. Part of a creek or shoreline was walled off to form a reservoir with an undershot wheel set in a gated sluice leading to the sea which would be attached to a mill house. The tidal flow would turn the wheel with more power available on the pool's release. One of the disadvantages of this system of water power was that the working hours of the miller were unsociable being controlled by the tide times.

Recent developments in tide and wave power have received a boost with the installation of a wave-hub in the sea off Hayle. This is a connection point that power generation experiments may join the National Grid.

Cornwall has never had many windmills, possibly because of too many gales, or maybe the more dependable water power was far easier to use. Apart from very early flimsy structures at least six substantial windmills were working in the 18th century. However we now have dozens of imposing wind generators of electricity creating heated debate all over the county. Their growth, spurred by lucrative Government grants, is continuing with even bigger and more powerful structures. There is doubt whether

they can, independent of subsidy, be profitable. The disadvantages are that they are a visual imposition being placed on the highest wind-swept hills, and sometimes of course, the wind doesn't blow!

From the early days of mining it was always known that the further down you ventured, the hotter it got. Poldice Mine had recorded an air temperature of 100 degrees F. at 200 fathoms into the killas, and in the granite Tresavean had 86 degrees at 264 fathoms. The water issuing from Wheal Clifford was measured at 125 degrees F. Geothermal experiments were started at Rosemanoes Quarry, near Penryn in 1977. This 'hot rocks' project received European and Government funding and was overseen by Camborne School of Mines. Using water pumped at high pressure down a bore hole at considerable depth the granite was sufficiently shattered to allow heated water to rise in an adjacent bore hole. Although a partial success, the ascending water was not quite hot enough to drive the turbines to the desired speed. Further work is currently being done to make geothermal energy production more efficient with The Eden Project, among others, showing a keen interest.

Solar panels have, until recently, been viewed as a small scale help to individual properties. However large scale installations are about to be made with Government backing

100

to establish 'solar parks'. A typical arrangement might see an array of 2m. high, ground mounted, photo-voltaic panels occupying an area of two football pitches.

Most people support the experi-mentation that might lead to more renewable sources of energy. Fossil fuels cannot last forever, while nu-clear sources have their dangerous waste disposal problems. Possibly renewable energy sources, despite the huge subsidies needed at present, may, together with a more efficient use of all energy, combine with existing methods in the future.

RESTORMEL CASTLE

According to Pevsner in his Build-ings of England, Cornwall, 1951, "By far the most perfect example of military architecture in Cornwall, and in its plan, one of the most consummate in England." The castle measures 110 feet internal diameter with an original height of 28 feet, with walls some 9 feet thick.

Near Lostwithiel, on the River Fowey, it is one of the four chief Norman castles of Cornwall. The others are Launceston, Tintagel and Trematon.

It only once saw serious action when Charles I's forces drove out the Parliamentarian forces during the Civil War. The castle was taken by Sir Richard Grenville, who had been the M.P. for Fowey, in a storming of 21st August 1644. But, for reasons that are not at all clear, the castle was in ruins by 1740.

Now the castle is a scheduled monument maintained by English Heritage. In 1999 'members' of the Cornish Stannary Parliament removed the, to them, offensively worded signs while objecting to the word 'English'. They demand-ed that they be replaced with the word 'Cornish' instead. Fines were imposed!

ROCHE ROCK

A fascinating, must visit, mini granite tor near the village that takes its name from the Rock (French – Roche) and is pro-nounced roach. Its interest lies within two spheres, the geological and the human.

First the geology. The rock is an altered granite outcrop pushed through the surrounding slates. It is composed of schorl – a mixture of quartz and black tourmaline crystals which was formed as a result of deep-seated changes to the granite in a process called tourmalinisation.

Secondly, built into the rock is an ancient oratory or chapel dedicated to St Michael and built in 1409. It has a lower room to house the chaplain or anchorite, with the chapel proper above. It is also a place of legend with Tregeagle (q.v.) making yet another of his appearances.

ROSELAND, The

The prefix ros is Cornish for a promontory. The Roseland is the promontory lying between the Fal estuary and the sea to the east. It is a beautiful, unspoilt area of quiet farmland, beaches, headlands and creeks. It is never crowded, having a small town in St Mawes (q.v.) and many picturesque villages. One of the advantages that The Roseland enjoys is its peacefulness, because not being on the way to anywhere, it has no through traffic.

The only debate is to where The Roseland begins. Some insist that it is made up only of the four parishes of St Just, St Gerrans, St Anthony and Philleigh, so putting the northern boundary somewhere on the line of the Ruan River estuary to Nare Head. But others, myself included, think that Tregony is the gateway and The Dodman its northern limit. This will include Veryan, Portloe, Caerhayes and Ruanlanihorne, all places that conform to The Roseland's charm.

ROYAL CORNWALL SHOW

One of the best attended and most friendly of the country's agricultural shows, The Royal Cornwall takes place each year over three days in June. On average 120,000 people attend to see, not just farming interests, but a whole range of displays – flowers, dogs, show jumping, fairground, cookery, crafts – and that's just a few.

The first show was in 1793 and soon after was organised by The Royal Cornwall Agricultural Association. Between the years 1827 and 1857 it was always held at Truro. It then was sited in a different location each year until 1960 when a permanent home was created at Wadebridge. The site has been steadily improved over the years with permanent roadways and buildings. For many Cornish people, town and country, The Royal Cornwall show is a not to be missed occasion.

RUGBY FOOTBALL

Rugby, Cornwall's national sport, has its roots in hurling (q.v.). Carew, in 1602, described two main types of the sport, one of which had bushes set as goals, and strategies involving passing the ball, marking and tackling. This game of hurling was very rough yet "the hurlers are bound to the observation of many laws."

The more organised rugby football, incidentally older than William Webb Ellis, was brought to Cornwall by college graduates and professionals. There is something in the Celtic make-up that encourages the general population to partake in the sport, so those few 'teachers' were soon in teams of fishermen, farmers, miners and others. *The West Briton* of 1884 reported, "Last year, for the first time, Cornwall met Devon at Football (in Cornwall 'football' is rugby) and got well beaten. This was almost inevitable . . . but the result was a determination on the part of the Cornish players to start a Union for the purpose of furthering the game in the County. Accordingly a meeting was called at Truro, which was attended by representatives of the clubs established at Hayle, Falmouth, Truro, Redruth and Bodmin." Rugby in Cornwall had become organised.

1908 saw Cornwall's first major triumph with a County Championship Final victory, 17 - 3, over Durham at Redruth in front of 17,000 spectators. As a reward Cornwall were invited to represent the country in the Olympic Games at the White City where they gained a silver medal being beaten by Australia 32 - 3.

It would be another 82 years before Cornwall won the County Championship again. At Twickenham this time, in April 1991 they beat Yorkshire 29 - 16 after extra time. Watched by a probable 40,000, the vast majority being Cornish cheering in black and gold, Twickenham had never before seen such enthusiasm in this competition. It was about much more than rugby football. Indeed after the 1989 final watched by over 20,000 setting the standard for county support, a reporter from *The Independent* wrote, "Twenty thousand Cornishmen used the great ground for a statement, if not of Celtic nationhood, then at least of their distinct identity." The Guardian went further, "the lusty spirit of national independence is alive and flourishing in the undeclared Republic of Cornwall." Unfortunately we just lost to Durham 13 - 9.

Cornish rugby is passionate with the county's men and women taking immense pride in their players and what they represent. The Camborne School of Mines supplied our first International in G. Gordon-Smith who played for England three times in 1900. He was followed by many others including five post war England captains in Vic Roberts, Keith Scott, John Kendall-Carpenter, Richard Sharp and Phil Vickery.

Modern rugby in the county is league based and at the top level professional. Before the 1990's many sides were of a similar standard enabling meaningful fixtures promoting local rivalries. In recent years a few clubs have dominated while others find their level in area leagues which can lead to the financial burdens of travel, this too also affects the

Cornwall v Gloucestershire, Rugby Football Union County Championships, 1999.

Photograph: Tobi Carver

big boys! At the time of writing Penzance (The Cornish Pirates) is the senior side with Redruth and Launceston next in line. Gates vary with the county side no longer able to attract the huge crowds of yester-day in a competition which the R.F.U. has pushed to one side. However one certainty remains in that Rugby Football is still very much in the hearts of the Cornish people.

S

SAFFRON CAKE

The Cornish people's fascination with saffron has led to arguments about origins. Some seem to want to bring those Phoenicians (q.v.) into the story again by suggesting that they traded saffron for tin. Why, when saffron was widely available all over England? Think of Saffron Walden in Essex which was just one centre for the saffron crocus culture. It is the dried stamens of a particular crocus that is saffron, most of which is now imported from Spain.

Until recent television inspired culinary trends, as well as an increase in Eastern cookery, the use of saffron tended to die out in Britain with the exception of Cornwall. Certainly the 'Cousin Jacks' took it to all parts of the mining world, occasionally having difficulty getting it through the post as it aroused suspicions as to whether it was a poison.

The saffron bun, or 'tea-treat' bun, was a regular at chapel gatherings and Sunday school treats or outings. Saffron was and still is very expensive and was sold by the dram. A common expression in Cornwall is 'as dear as saffron.'

This typical recipe comes from the Lostwithiel W.I. of 1929.

"Take 2 lbs. of flour, 1 lb. fat (lard, butter or a mixture), ¼ lb. sugar, 2 oz. mixed peel, 1 lb. currants or sultanas, or mixed, 1 oz. yeast, warm milk.

Rub fat thoroughly into flour and sugar, add good pinch of salt. Put yeast in a cup with teaspoonful of sugar, add little warm milk – not hot, but more than tepid. When yeast rises in cup make a pit in flour and pour the yeast in, turn a little flour over it. When this cracks and the yeast sponges through, mix into a soft dough with the hand, using milk as required. Add saffron when mixing. Add fruit, put a warm plate on it and stand it in a warm place until the mixture raises the plate and appears light and spongy. Allow to 'rise' for a short time before baking.

To prepare saffron, take half drachm (sic) and cut very fine with scissors, pour over ½ cup boiling water and steep over night."

SAINTS AND HOLY WELLS

Cornwall probably has more Saints' names in towns and villages than anywhere else in Britain. The original foundations of the Cornish Church were about a thousand or more years ago. These little orato-

105

ries, places to pray, were very crude buildings of which the remains of two are known today, one at Gwithian and the other in the dunes of Perranzabuloe. Both had the driven sand to cover and protect them and both have had recent histories of cover or uncover policies of preservation. The St Piran's Oratory is one of the oldest stone built places of worship in the country being over 1,400 years old.

These and many other countywide were established by the Christian Saints or Missionaries who came from other Celtic centres like Wales, Brittany and Ireland. Legend has them arriving in all manner of impossible ways, like St Ya (Eia) of St Ives on a leaf and St Piran on a millstone!

Although Cornwall was nominally Christian there was still a strong pagan influence which the Saints had to overcome. It was usual for the Missionaries to work around the heathen beliefs to the Christian good, as for example, consecrating wells as holy that had previously been known to have magical powers. J Henry Harris in his Cornish Saints and Sinners, 1905, sums up the holy wells. "Wherever there was a well a saint took possession of it. The votive offerings of the natives to the bright, sparkling divinity dwelling in springs of water passed into their hands, the water cures became 'miracles', and chapels and baptistries were built over the wells. Chapels and hermits' cells abound. There

is one spring which insures a man from hanging if he is but christened with its water in childhood. There is another, in which a madman may be ducked until he is cured; there is another, in which a maiden may see her 'future', and there are others which can cure sad souls and sadder bodies."

With the building of the churches as we know them today came the dedication to a saint already established in the area.

ST AGNES

St Agnes, or St Anns in the vernacular, is one of Cornwall's most honest and historic villages. Close to the sea, and yet not dominated by it, St Agnes was at the centre of a rich mining area, especially in the 19th century.

At Trevaunance Cove fishing has always taken place while the remains of a harbour can be seen under the western cliff. In this very exposed situation this 19th century structure was gone by 1930. Its primary purpose was to load small ships with tin and copper ores for other ports. The beach offers good surfing and is the base for an inshore lifeboat, first installed by the television programme 'Blue Peter'. Cornwall's first seal sanctuary was established here in the 1950's by Ken Jones, later expanding to a new site at Gweek.

Trevaunance Cove was not always so appealing. Mining was

having its impact when Folliott-Stokes visited in the 1920's, "On the beach itself a great overshot wheel revolves, and discharges dirty water on to the already discoloured sand, on the hills above are more wheels, slowly moving chains, much heaps, and smoking chimneys; while the loud and ceaseless clatter of stamps fills the air with noise."

The village has more than its fair share of folklore and superstition. We have already met the giant (q.v.) Bolster who could step from St Agnes Beacon to Carn Brea. The story of Dorcas concerns Polbreen Mine at the foot of the Beacon. Dorcas, who lived in an adjoining cottage, became so depressed that she threw herself into a mineshaft. Her broken body was found and she was later buried. But her spirit remained in the mine as a ghost, taunting the miners and interrupting their work. If a tributer (see Mining) had had a poor month producing little, he would be asked if he had been 'chasing Dorcas'? On one rare occasion she apparently acted benevolently by calling the name of a miner continually until he came to look. Seconds later a rock fall occurred which would have crushed him had he not moved. To his dying day the miner said that he owed his life to Dorcas.

A little bit of leg-pulling, similar to a story told in Towednack, concerns the cuckoo. An attempt was made to capture and keep the seasonal visitor. By all accounts the attempt was nearing a successful conclusion. Having hedged it in to prevent escape the bird flew over the top to the disappointed remark, "One more tob (turf) an we'd av ad un!"

ST AUSTELL

Cornwall's largest town by population is the administrative centre of the china clay industry. But it is too easy to forget how near to the sea St Austell is. There are many beaches, ports and harbours within the confines of St Austell Bay.

The town grew in the 18th century from what was really only a village. The rapid development later coming from the fortunes of china clay following the demise of tin and copper mining in the area.

Within the town the church deserves a mention with its fine 15th century tower enriched on all four sides by figure sculptures set in niches. The old Market House is also worth a visit.

Overlooking the town is the home of a family business that continues to do well, The St Austell Brewery. Founded by Walter Hicks in 1851, it is Cornwall's leading brewer with some 140 pubs, inns and hotels in Cornwall, Devon, Somerset and the Isles of Scilly. The 'real' ale, Tribute, is a favourite being guested all over the country.

The much lauded Eden Project (q.v.) is only a short distance away.

ST IVES

Named from Saint Ya (Ia or Eia) pronounced as two syllables, it was at one time called Porthia. St Ya was a female who arrived from Ireland on a leaf! The church, which was built from 1410 looks especially good when viewed from the water when its four gabled ends spread out in pride. There are many chapels in the town paying homage to St Ives' strong Methodist traditions. On top of the promontory known as The Island is a small simple chapel dedicated to St Nicholas.

Historically the economy of St Ives was based on fishing and mining, but now tourism is king. In a Black's Guide to Cornwall of 1874 it is "to be regretted that the favourable impression which at first the tourist necessarily forms, should be dissipated on his entrance into the town by the accumulation of nastiness. The streets are narrow and crooked, the houses old and shattered, the shops mean and squalid, and everywhere pervades a fishy smell, most intolerable and not to be endured." No doubt now, guides will delight in streets narrow and crooked, and oh the chance to smell a real fresh fish! St Ives is certainly a jewel, with beautiful and varied beaches, a delightful harbour and with wonderfully scenic surroundings.

St Ives' natives are very proud of their fishing heritage which encompassed many types of operation and the catching of numerous species. The seining for pilchards (q.v.) was especially frenetic. The fishermen lived 'Downalong', the low lying area of cottages, fish cellars and sail lofts. 'Upalong' was more likely to have, among others, miners and mine workers. In either to say, "Hello Mr Stevens." had a good chance of success.

The nickname 'Hakes' comes from the story of the fishermen being fed up with catching hake instead of more favoured species. An individual hake was flogged on the sands before being returned to the sea to tell the others! Hence St Ives where they flogged the hake.

See St Ives Artists and Lifeboats.

The Island, St Ives

108

ST IVES' ARTISTS

Cornwall has always attracted artists. A combination of good light, climate, the sea and moors, together with a quieter life and tranquillity all contributed to productive art. In St Ives artists could paint people at work, being accepted by the community at large and soon an artists' colony grew up. Sail lofts and fish cellars were becoming available thus creating perfect studios, cheap to rent.

Ben Nicholson arrived in 1939. His abstract art was inspired by his surroundings, "it's like walking through the country from St Ives to Zennor." If you have done that, then you too know inspiration! Similarly abstract painter Terry Frost gained inspiration from the harbour, "it was not portraying the boats, the sand, the horizon ..... but concentrating on the emotion engendered by what I see. The subject matter is in fact the sensation evoked by the movements and the colour in the harbour." Peter Lanyon too was fired by the Celtic atmosphere around him when he came to St Ives in 1918.

Sven Berlin was a colourful, larger than life, sculptor, but most famous was Barbara Hepworth, internationally famous, and deeply under the influence of natural Cornwall.

Alfred Wallis, a former fisherman, turned to primitive painting at the age of 70. He would use house paint on old pieces of board to create naive art that today is in great demand. In a similar vein, and yet in so totally different circumstances, is

A Hepworth

the work of Bryan Pearce. A sufferer of a debilitating mental condition, his art is simplistic and at the same time fascinating.

Bernard Leach founded a pottery here in 1920. He was a master potter of world renown, partly influenced by Japanese techniques, producing exquisite stoneware.

Troika Pottery, now much in demand, was set up by Benny Sirota, Leslie Ilsley and Jan Thompson at Wheal Dream in the early 60's.

The Tate St Ives exhibits modern English art as well as works of the St Ives School. Built on the site of an old gasworks, overlooking Porthmeor beach, it was opened in 1993 with hopes of expansion.

ST JUST

Cornwall has two St Justs, the larger in West Penwith and the smaller on the Roseland. (q.v.)

St Just down west is one of Cornwall's most genuine small towns. It is a strong, squat granite settlement, not far from Land's End, with a history based on mining. The St Just miner was a strong independent worker. In most other mining areas pairs worked together, one holding the borer, and another the hammer. But not so here, "Our men work single handed. They hold the borer with one hand and beat with the other, and when the hand gets tired with the hammer the man changes it. That is a reason why the eastern men cannot work here with our men." (Parliamentary Papers 1864) Nearby were the mines of Botallack and Levant (q.v.) famed in mining history.

One of Cornwall's 'playing places' (q.v.), an open air theatre is to be found here. In this plein an gwarry Cornish miracle plays were performed. St Just men are fiercely proud of their town and are keen sportsmen, especially in rugby and cricket. Nearby is Land's End Airport, a setting off point for Scilly.

St Just-in-Roseland Church

St Just in Roseland is most famous for its church, beautifully situated above a creek of the River Fal estuary and surrounded by exotic gardens. The little creek is a haven for small craft while the signpost from the main road causes amusement with the inscription 'St Just Church and Bar'.

ST MAWES

St Mawes was not always the prosperous, south facing haven of fine houses and hotels that it is today. Once relying on fishing and some boat-building, it then gradually became a place of leisure, holidays and retirement for the comfortably off.

A clergyman writing about St Mawes some 200 years ago described it as, "A mean village with no house of God in it, and few houses fit for the residence of men."

The quay, although renovated many times, is at least 500 years old and was the centre for fish and trade.

Much is made of the continental feel to this small town. The Blue Book Guide to Cornwall of the 50's goes a little over the top, as guidebooks can, "St Mawes with its harbour, little buildings sprawling around the peninsula, and its artists, is a kind of British edition of St Tropez on the Riviera. Many people say it is like Capri. The atmosphere and setting of this exquisite fishing village is informal

St Mawes Castle

and delightful and is one of the quaintest, happiest and still unspoilt holiday haunts in England." I bet you can't wait to go there!

St Mawes is certainly not typically Cornish, and is unlike any other coastal village in the county, with the possible exception of Rock. At present it still has some fishing but it is essentially a resort for those who can afford it.

For St Mawes Castle, see Pendennis.

ST MICHAEL'S MOUNT & MARAZION

The home of the St Aubyn family since the mid 17th century, it now belongs to The National Trust. The island is said by some to be the Ictis of long ago where tin was traded and exported. There is some positive opinion on this but there is no certainty. This granite outcrop was the site of a Benedictine Chapel established by Edward the Confessor as a cell of the Norman Mont St Michel which it strongly resembles. Of the chapel, only a rock chamber below what is now the chapel survives. The monastery was rebuilt from 1135 by Bernard, Abbot of Mont St Michel. According to Pevsner in his Buildings of England, Cornwall, 1951 "The community on the Mount was suppressed in 1425 as alien and King Henry VI gave the property to his favourite Brigittine Nuns of Syon, near London. After the Reformation it belonged to the Kings who had their appointed Governors there. In the 17th century it changed hands three times, first to the Earl of Salisbury, then to Francis Basset of Tehidy and finally c1660 to the St Aubyns."

On the island's base is a small collection of cottages by a small harbour. The construction of the causeway and the harbour started in the 15th century, with a rebuild in 1727 by Sir John St Aubyn. In the late 19th century the village had over fifty houses, together with shops, a school, a bakery, a pub and a chapel. It had a thriving trade in tin and copper ores, with imports of Scandinavian timber. Today the cottages house the people who work there with other buildings catering for the thousands of daily visitors. St Michael's Mount is one of the most visited of the National Trust's properties.

Opposite the Mount is the little town of Marazion. In Cornish

Marazion means little market, which is exactly what it was in medieval times when compared with its very near neighbour Market Jew (Thursday Market). The two places had merged by 1600.

See Giants.

ST PIRAN

The patron saint, not of Cornwall, although he seems to have been adopted as such, but of the Cornish miners (tinners).

In Ireland St Piran, possibly Ciaran, had worked miracles for the Irish kings, but despite his goodness three kings condemned him to be cast off a cliff into the sea with a millstone around his neck. Robert Hunt's Popular Romances of the West of England, 1871, takes up the story, "The winds were blowing tempestuously, the heavens were dark with clouds, and the waves white with crested foam. No sooner was Piran and the millstone launched into space, then the sun shone out brightly, casting the full lustre of its beams on the holy man, who sat tranquilly on the descending stone. The winds died away, and the waves became smooth as a mirror. The moment the millstone touched the water, hundreds were converted to Christianity who saw this miracle. St Piran floated on safely to Cornwall, he landed on 5th March on the sands which bear his name. He lived amongst the Cornish men until he attained the age of 206 years."

To set a time for St Piran is not easy, but let's say about 1,500 years ago. (Bishop Usher, who once calculated the age of the Earth by the literal mathematics of the Bible, put St Piran's birth at 352 A.D.) So he certainly was not the first to discover or smelt tin! The miners, however adopted him as their saint. His day, 5th March, was a day off to celebrate with many becoming "as drunk as a Perranner". This holiday died out in the early 1800's, but in recent years St Piran's Day has attracted many to celebrate with treks across Perran Sands to his Oratory and Cross. His flag, the white upright cross on a black background, tentatively said by some to indicate the white tin in the black tinstone mass, is now found countywide and is taken on important trips up-country to proudly show who we are.

St Piran, or if you prefer Perran, gives his name to several Cornish locations. His home parish, Perranzabuloe means Perran in the sands. Perranporth is of-course Perran's cove. Perranarworthal is Perran of the manor of Arworthal. Perranuthnoe is Perran in the manor of Uthno. And Perranwell is self-explanatory.

SECOND HOMES

Be within sight, sound or a sniff of the sea and there you will find the second home. Less will you find the residence of a man for whom the sea provides a living, but more for a man whose living is or was in some far-flung city. A village lucky enough to have developed in beautiful surroundings because of a need to house the people who scraped a living from the sea or the land around it is now a village where such people can rarely afford to dwell. Tiny, rough and ill-equipped houses that would have seen large families raised generation after generation, have now become quaint cottages, desirable, with microwave and shower, where neither infant cries nor Cornish voices are heard.

The second home is not a modern phenomenon. By 1926 Veryan Parish Council needed to provide houses for the working classes "since a large number of houses are being used as summer residences and houses are urgently needed for fishermen." This is Portloe where second homes now dominate. As at many other Cornish coastal communities the only available building sites were away from the coves and harbours, and because of the typical Cornish topography this meant near or on the top of hills. This would lead to a long up-hill trudge, just what the hard-working fisherman needed at the end of a long day!

The high demand for a holiday home in a desirable location has always inflated house prices, and as a consequence put the properties out of reach of many people, especially the younger generation. These houses are no longer 'affordable', to use a modern, annoyingly indefinite term. So we find that generations of village families die out because of the need of the youngest having to leave. Families who in the past shaped, gave character and life to the community.

Occupation of the second home is usually confined to the summer months so that the resident shopkeeper or publican has to struggle for more than six months of the year in a graveyard of a winter. Schools cannot survive the loss of the generations who would have provided them with a succession of pupils.

Despite promises by Governments, especially when in opposition, to tackle the problem, either nothing of substance is done or perhaps nothing can be done. The homes can be divided into two types. Those that when the owners are not in residence, no one is, and those that are regularly let out. At least the latter provide a few customers for the village. Perhaps you have a solution?

SHELTER BOX

A Cornwall based humanitarian charity that has received much acclaim and a great deal of local support. Founded by ex Royal

Navy diver Tom Henderson in April 2000 Shelter Box gets tents and basic equipment to where ever in the world, through disaster, natural or manmade, creates a need. The organisation is through the Rotary Club of the Helston-Lizard area with its headquarters in the former.

Within days of a need a shipment of boxes is on its way, not just from Helston, but from emergency depots worldwide. Over the last few years many thousands of boxes have been deployed to every continent with relief from earthquakes, tsunami, floods, typhoons, hurricanes, volcanic eruptions and conflict. All funding is by charitable donation.

SMUGGLING

The lot of the Cornish fisherman, and indeed the miner, was one of hard work in difficult conditions for little financial reward. In such conditions to indulge in 'fair trade' was a natural development to raise a living standard from what could only be described as near poverty. Smuggling was not for the mere love of adventure or a desire to get one over on the Revenue Authorities. Like 'wrecking' (q.v.), smuggling helped provide an income of money or kind, and with conscience clear the men were free-traders above any manmade law.

"It is impossible" declared Lord Holland in a speech before The House of Lords, 9th July 1805, "totally to prevent smuggling. All that the Legislature can do is to compromise with a crime which, whatever laws may be made to constitute it a high offence, the mind of man can never conceive as at all equalling in turpitude those acts which are breaches of clear moral virtues." His thoughts were somewhat echoed by Adam Smith in his definition of a smuggler as "a person who, though no doubt highly blameable for violating the laws of his country, is frequently incapable of violating those of natural justice, and who would have been in every respect an excellent citizen had not the laws of his country made that a crime which Nature never meant it to be so."

Perhaps as a Cornishman I have painted a picture from a one-eyed viewpoint. So I must not ignore the fact that smuggling did have its dark side. Let Dr Johnson's definition of a smuggler redress the balance. "A wretch who, in defiance of justice and the laws, imports or exports goods either contraband or without payment of the Customs."

The smuggler had an obvious enemy in the Excisemen and the Coastguard. Fearing not only the loss of valuable trade on capture, the punishment for the offence was severe. Often the big time smuggler would be armed, sometimes with an arsenal considerably more powerful than side-arms. The contraband, having been distributed inland, would be fiercely defended

114

by ruthless men. More than one Customs' Officer had been killed while going about their duty.

Whereas 'wrecking' provided material directly of use to the poor, smuggling on the other hand supplied the whole of the community from pauper to publican, and from parson to squire. The necessity of sharing 'trade' made a link between all parties. The owner of the vessel had to evade the Revenue cutter while at sea and dispose of the contraband before arriving at his own port, sometimes by anchoring kegs so that in a submerged state they could be grapnelled up later when the coast was clear. Once ashore the goods had to be hidden, usually in the homes of obliging persons, possibly farmers, or even the local squire. At all times there being played out a cat and mouse game with authority.

In Mylor Churchyard is a tombstone to Thomas James, killed while returning from a 'fishing trip', 7th December 1814. It shows the strong feelings aroused in the area by the death of this thirty-five year old.

We have not a moment we can call our own
Officious zeal in luckless hour laid wait
And wilful sent the murderous ball of Fate!
James to his home, which late in health he left
Wounded returns – of life is soon bereft.

STANNARIES, The

In 1194 King Richard I was in France at war. One area of fundraising concerned the Cornish tin industry. It was seen over by William de Wrotham, entitled Warden of the Stannaries, in other words Supremo of anything to do with tin production! Assisted by jurors of tinners, codes of practice became 'law' in the regulation of tin sales, including weights and measures. Ancient privileges were maintained concerning 'digging for tin' and the taking of fuel for smelting without hindrance.

With the control of tin being most important, a charter set out stannary areas in the county within which the miner was subject to Stannary Law, in a similar way to soldiers being under military law. Miners were free to search for tin ore with only a few restrictions on enclosed land. A further privilege enjoyed by the Cornish miner was to have their disputes heard and tried in their own Stannary Courts, this apart from very serious crimes.

The tinner was also exempt from ordinary taxation but at times national need was often petitioned by high ranking politicians. In 1597 even the Queen appealed to the tinners for help in financing warfare at Cadiz.

Exemption was even made from any military summons. The balance was somewhat redressed by the coinage system. At various coinage towns taxes were imposed on all tin smelted in that district. Liskeard and Lostwithiel served the eastern stannaries, with Truro and Helston, and later Penzance, serving the west. A small corner (coin) of each 320 lb. block was removed and assayed for quality. If everything was in order and the tax paid, the block would receive an official hammered stamp of the Duchy Arms.

SURFING

Up to fifty or so years ago surfing was known as surf-riding. A very popular recreation for the summer months where a person in a bathing costume would lie on a flat wooden board, somewhat resembling an ironing board top, and a little shorter than themselves. From within their own depth they would launch themselves at a soon learned split second

before the next wave was about to break, or in good conditions, had already broken. The board was not supportive of the person's weight, but acted rather like a water ski.

The Blue Book Guide to Cornwall of 1958 says in its section on Newquay, headed Surf Bathing, "The Atlantic rollers provide the finest opportunities in the country for enjoying this exciting and exhilarating sport. For thousands of visitors the surfboard is high on their holiday packing list, but it can always be hired from the beaches or bought in the town."

It was all change in the 60's when foreign, chiefly Australian, lifeguards became employed at Cornwall's major north coast resorts. In 1962 large Malibu boards of fibreglass construction started to appear, brought over for the lifeguards' recreational use. Soon after, together with surfers from Jersey, the British Surfing Association was formed leading to a new organised sport. The sport mushroomed with local board manufacture and the introduction of the neoprene wetsuit allowing for all year round surfing for those keen enough. Organised competition flourished with many involving an international field and the appearance of the surfing professional. The Cornish surfing industry contributes much to the county's economy with the unbeatable Fistral Beach at its centre.

SURNAMES

By the Middle Ages surnames were used to distinguish between people who had the same personal forenames. As people moved about more freely, it was necessary to identify which John was being talked about, and then to continue a surname for the family to come.

Surnames can mostly be categorised into one of four groups. The original place of residence – Greenwood, Kent or Hill. The father's name – Johnson (Johns), Rogers or Davidson. A trade – Baker, Shipwright or Smith. A characteristic – Long, Armstrong or Redhead (Read). Cornish surnames can be arranged in the same four groups.

"By Tre, Pol, Ros or Pen. You may know most Cornishmen."

Not quite, only those in the first group. Tre is a homestead, Pol a pool, Ros a heath or promontory, Pen a head or end.

Examples: Trelawney, Tregunna, Tredinnick, Polglaze, Polkinhorn, Polmear, Roskrow, Rosevear, Rosewarne, Pengelly, Penhaligon, Penna

Many other Cornish situations became surnames – Bray a hill, Hosking a marsh, Hendy an old house, Hendra an old town, Chenoweth a new house, Nancarrow a valley of deer.

From father's name we have, Blamey a form of Bellamy, Clemo of Clement, Ellis of Elli (Eli).

From trades or positions: Angove a smith, Tyack a peasant farmer, Dyer a thatcher and Rule a chief.

From characteristics: Annear is tall, Angwin is fair, Kemp is neat or tidy and Prout is proud.

It would seem that most Cornish surnames are from homes, farms, hamlets or villages. The initial need to identify people came from the immediate vicinity, and then from parish to parish, so one doesn't find a John Redruth or a Luke Penryn. If a person travelled beyond the county into a 'foreign' land, he would be known as John from Kernow or Cornish John. so becoming John Curnow (Kernow) or John Cornish. John Cornwall is not common.

T

TAMAR, The River

Prime Minister David Cameron said, in October 2010, concerning a possible cross-border constituency, a form of 'Devonwall', "It's the Tamar, not the Amazon for Heaven's sake!" Does he not realise what this flowing natural frontier means to the Cornish? The feelings that arise in crossing it to leave home, and the feelings on the return?

The boundary is not just geographical but also involves personality and make up. W Gore Allen, editor of *The Devon Journal*, once wrote, "Whenever I cross the Tamar, I am surprised afresh that one of the world's least penetrable frontiers should be made evident by so small a width of water. Cornwall and Devon could send plenipotentiaries almost to clasp hands across the stream: yet if these men were truly representative of their two counties they would turn away, the Cornish choleric, the Devon men resigned to admit their mutual and complete incomprehension. The differences are mental, spiritual and emotional."

Of the river itself, its source is nearly 60 miles north of Plymouth, and about 4 miles from the Atlantic. It has been our natural boundary for centuries, although historically there have been a few minor blips of incursion from Devon. Its Cornish tributaries include the rivers Inny, Ottery, Kensey and Lynher. The Tamar has a good salmon population while its valley's agriculture was noted for fruit and spring flower production.

At Calstock there is a magnificent viaduct taking the railway from Gunnislake down to Plymouth. At one time there was an impressive wagon lift allowing trucks to be taken up and down to and from the track on the busy quay. On both sides of the river many minerals were extracted, including copper and tin with silver being produced in sufficient quantities to be able to supply The Mint.

Cotehele, home of the Earl of Mount Edgcumbe, now owned by The National Trust. has an interesting quay with a restored trading vessel, *The Shamrock*. Passing Pentillie with its castle, and Landulph, the Tamar slowly widens until the two magnificent Saltash bridges come into view. Brunel's impressive Royal Albert Bridge, opened in 1859, is still a wonder today while the suspension road bridge of 1961 with its 1,100 feet span and sea clearance of 135 feet provides a good contrast. Saltash is Cornwall's oldest borough with a waterside of interest that before the road bridge had a chain ferry link to the Plymouth side.

Further south, and still a ferry link, is Torpoint, a crossing to Devonport. To see the lower Tamar in an enjoyable round trip, why not travel from Plymouth by train to Calstock? Then return to the Barbican by steamer. You'll get the best of both worlds.

TIN

Tin is a bright, white metal element Sn, having both malleable and ductile properties. It has a low melting point of only 232 degrees C. In Cornwall it is mainly found in the oxide form cassiterite or tinstone. The former is obtained from alluvial deposits as well as in lodes. Alluvial tin was the first to be claimed in Cornwall where it was 'streamed'. Large quantities of tin-bearing sands were mechanically shaken on special tables where the heavier tin ore remained as the lighter grains were washed away. It was economic to obtain only 1 kilo of black tin ore per tonne of sand. This source of tin, cheap to extract in countries like Malaya (Malaysia), led to immense pressure on the mines of the County.

In lodes, tin is often associated with arsenic, copper, iron and wolfram (tungsten ore). The higher costs of obtaining the ore from mines is in some ways offset by the greater concentration of tin. But as in every commercial activity the price received for the metal, allied with its supply and demand, determines who can profitably produce it.

Today tin is mainly produced in Malaysia, China, Bolivia, Indonesia and Russia. Hopefully, with the rising price for the metal, Cornwall may find a way to production again.

The uses of tin include tinplate, i.e. sheet iron with a very thin coating of tin as in tin cans. A number of important alloys include pewter, solder, bearing metals, bronze, gun metal and bell metal. Tin salts are used in printing and dying, and the ceramics industry.

TORREY CANYON DISASTER

Under the Liberian flag, and with an Italian crew, the 61,263 ton oil tanker *Torrey Canyon* was one of the world's largest ships. Early on the morning of 18th March 1967 it was high tide at Land's End as the ship made her way from the Persian Gulf with 118,000 tons of crude oil. In good weather and sea conditions the crew of the Seven Stones Lightship saw her steaming at about 17 knots straight for the reef. Warning rockets were fired, but to no avail. At 8.30 a.m. the 974 feet long ship ploughed into the granite rocks gashing her hull, ten of the eighteen tanks were holed. The oil began to spill to become the largest slick in history.

The crew were easily picked up the next day. The St Mary's Lifeboat took off 22 with the rest going by helicopter, except for Captain Rigiotti and 3 others, together with 2 from the Dutch tug *Utrecht*.

Within two days the oil slick was 18 miles long and 2 miles wide. Salvage attempts were to prove useless. A wind change pushed the black tide to the Cornish coast, while the Isles of Scilly remained clear. By 26th March the ship had broken her back. A Cabinet Meeting was called by Prime Minister, Harold Wilson, declaring the west a battle zone with 600 troops sent to clear up the mess. Eight Buccaneer aircraft bombed the wreck with Hunter jets following on with incendiaries attempting to burn off the remaining crude. By now the oil had reached Devon on both coasts. Much debate raged in the ensuing years as to which caused the more environmental damage, the oil or the chemicals sprayed to disperse it. For wildlife it was a disaster that took years to come right.

TOURISM

The early visitor to Cornwall tended to be comfortably off with plenty of time to travel and explore. They needed to be fit to cope with the lack of transport that today we take for granted. Some came with the intention of recording their experiences for publication.

Celia Fiennes, 1698, travelled the length of the county for her 'Through England on a Side-saddle in the Time of William and Mary'. When she arrived at the market town of St Austin (St Austell) she tells how her landlady brought her cream. "They scald their cream and milk, and so it is a form of clouted (sic) cream, as we call it, and so put it on the top of the apple pie."

Daniel Defoe, best remembered for his 'Robinson Crusoe', compiled 'A Tour Through the Whole Island of Great Britain', 1724 - 27. On Scilly he upset the natives by claiming that those wrecked on the Islands "find the rocks themselves not more merciless than the people who range about them for their prey."

Author Wilkie Collins, who wrote 'The Woman in White', came to Cornwall where he wrote of his travels in 'Rambles Beyond Railways', 1851. Of his reception he writes, "The manners of the Cornish of all ranks, down to the lowest, are remarkably distinguished by courtesy – a courtesy of that kind which is quite independent of artificial breeding, and which proceeds solely from natural motives of kindness and from an innate anxiety to please. Few of the people pass you without a salutation."

A Frenchman called Henri-Alphonse Esquiros wrote 'Cornwall and its Coast' in 1865. At Bude he was inspired to write, "Stern promontories Compass Point and

Beacon Hill spread out wide shadows over the stern waves of the Atlantic. In calm weather this bay is delicious, the sea at high tide advances describing foaming semicircles, which enlarge and become appeased as they invade the beach; but let a west wind begin to blow, and the spectacle at once changes, just as wild horses take to flight before a prairie fire, the impetuous coursers of the ocean, so the sailors say, escape from the presence of these terrible winds with a loud snorting, and rush back towards the barrier of cliffs."

A.G. Folliott-Stokes in his 'The Cornish Coast and Moors', 1928, meticulously covered every inch of the shore and writing about Porthtowan, "We descended by a steep path into Porthtowan Cove. There is a broad strip of sand here, towering headlands, and a stream much impregnated with iron. This is one of the playgrounds of the Redruthians. There are numerous little teasheds on the shore, and this afternoon the sands are bright with scores of paddling children."

With the growing of the touring interest came the Tourist Guides. Some were extremely detailed and many were brutally honest about places that never ever expected to be on the tourist's trail. It must be remembered that towns which are now considered tourist centres may have earlier been dominated by industry. As a good example let us consider Hayle.

Murray's Handbook of Devon and Cornwall, 1859, has Hayle as "having no pretensions as a town. It consists chiefly of mean cottages, a few poor shops, an inn, and a shabby railway viaduct, and overall whitewash and coal dust seem to struggle for the mastery. It is however a busy port and the coast in the neighbourhood is most beautiful."

Black's Guide to Cornwall of 1874 seems to revel in its nastiness. "A dirtier, squalider, less interesting town than Hayle is not to be found in all Cornwall. Its population is composed of fishermen and miners, of labourers in its two foundries or tin smelting works, and railway employees, and its only claim to consideration is its position with respect to some magnificent coast scenery. But this may almost as easily be visited from Redruth or St Ives, and therefore we recommend the tourist to imitate our own course of action – leave Hayle as quickly as he enters it!"

By the 1920's Hayle's industry was waning and its tourism was becoming of greater interest, as can be appreciated from 'Cornwall – England's Riviera, 1926, "Hayle, a busy commercial town with possibilities as a seaside resort. It is a seaport, possesses foundries, rope works, timber yards, breweries, etc. . . . but it also possesses in the towans, stretching to the Gwithian Sands and the North Cliffs, an immense playground of sand hills, flanked at the water's edge by a lengthy sandy beach affording several miles of bathing."

So now we are into the bucket and spade holidays with an emphasis on the beach. Into the 50's the 'Blue Book Guide to Cornwall', 1958, shows Hayle in an altogether different light. Gone is most of the town's industry, so now "the situation of Hayle as a holiday centre is excellent, and for exploring south-west Cornwall it is unrivalled. The railway station is central and the train service and the road motoring arrangements good."

We have already encountered the first, almost professional, tourists. The greatest influence that followed was the coming of the railway in the mid 1800's. Now a faster means of transportation than horses was available. Although not cheap, it enabled tourists to come from further a field in a reasonable time. Places to stay grew up around the stations with many a 'Railway Hotel' or 'Station Guest House' making an appearance. Holiday breaks could now be scheduled around a railway timetable, perhaps offering extra local trips.

The areas of the county not served by rail had to wait until motoring became more common, firstly for the comfortably off and by the mid 50's to a whole new motoring population.

A further change took place with the appearance of the workers' annual holidays. Whole factories, especially in the Midlands, would shut down production with thousands seeking a holiday, mostly by train, to the seaside. Even a branch line like the one to St Ives could have a weekend train of up to thirteen carriages squeezing into the little station. Newquay station witnessed similar scenes. Now came the age of the Bed and Breakfast landlady and the ice cream cornet tourist. Not so much touring but mainly sitting tight with a limited budget. Of course some resorts still specialised with an upmarket clientele, mostly those remote from the railway track as, for example, St Mawes.

With the new age of motoring the caravan made an appearance with farmers and landowners now cultivating a new crop – campers and caravanners! By the 60's Cornwall was almost full, helped by Harold Wilson's Government's limit on money being taken out of the country. A bonus to fight the new cheap packaged foreign holiday that would come to have a huge influence.

The visitors that still came had to be looked after in poor weather as well as good. So the last few decades have seen a mushrooming of 'visitor attractions', some good, others more dubious, all existing to keep the tills ringing whatever the weather.

A new initiative has seen the arrival of several large cruise ships to Cornish ports each unloading hundreds of extra visitors to help maintain one of Cornwall's vital industries. Like it or loath it, we would struggle without our visitors.

TREGEAGLE

He pops up in Cornish folklore and legend in all sorts of places. The wretched soul is always undergoing some punishing curse or attempting impossible tasks. In violent storms he is heard to howl or whistle through the dark woods chased by devil dogs. Tregeagle was supposed to have been a wealthy and powerful man but wicked. Some say he was a murderer, but all say that his spirit haunts many locations county-wide.

One such place is Dozmary (Dosmare) Pool on Bodmin Moor. In the legend John Tregeagle is a Head Steward to Lord Robartes of Lanhydrock, or some say a Steward to the Earl of Radnor, who was ordered to empty the Pool with a

limpet shell! Some say that the shell even had a hole in it! Tregeagle the 'Headless Hunter' with hounds from Hell is still heard on the Moor. He travels from Dozmary Pool to Roche Rock (q.v.) looking for sanctuary, but none is found there. This verse is from a poem in J Henry Harris's Cornish Saints and Sinners, 1906.

Back o'er the moor, the frozen moor,
Flies the curst soul to Dozmary Pool.
With gleaming fangs and eyes aflame,
The pack, the pack, the hellish pack
Race by his side, yap, yap, yap –
Race by the side of the soul in pain.
Back to the Pool, the frozen pool,
The burning soul, the notable soul,
Flies to its prison of tears, hot tears,
Flies to its curst prison of tears,
The soul of Tregeagle in pain.

Some legends have Tregeagle spinning sand into rope, and at the Loe Bar (q.v.) moving sand from one end to the other. He represents a universal figure forever facing the eternal consequences of sinning. Poor chap!

TRELAWNY, BISHOP

Who was this man that we sing about at county rugby matches? Although we only sing the first verse, few know the rest. Did he live or die? And were there really 20,000 Cornishmen wanting to know the reason why?

Sir John Trelawny was born at Trelawne in Pelynt in 1650. He became a bishop some time after

Dozmary Pool

123

studying at Oxford University and after holding various church posts. He and other bishops petitioned against King James II's Declaration of Indulgence of 1687 which granted religious tolerance to Catholics. Charged with seditious libel he and others were imprisoned in the Tower of London. They protested that although they were in support of the King, they did not think that Catholics, even in their own homes, should have the freedom to worship in their way. After three weeks Trelawny was tried and acquitted, leading to great celebrations in his home parish of Pelynt.

Bishop Trelawny was immortalised in the adopted Cornish anthem entitled 'The Song of the Western Men'. This was written by the noted Parson Stephen Hawker of Morwenstow.

And shall Trelawny live?
Or shall Trelawny die?
Here's twenty thousand Cornish men
Will know the reason why!

Hawker wrote the song, some six verses of it, in 1824. 136 years after the event! In fact the march to have him released only got as far as Bristol before news of the acquittal became known.

Cornish historian Morton Nance has suggested that Hawker was influenced by an earlier song 'Come all ye jolly tinner boys', written in response to Napoleon's threats that might affect the tin trade. That song contained the line, *'Why forty thousand Cornish boys shall know the reason why'*.

TRENGROUSE, HENRY

Henry Trengrouse from Helston invented a rocket apparatus for saving life from shipwrecks. In December 1807 he witnessed the grounding of the frigate Anson on the Loe Bar during a fierce gale. The crew's attempts at making the shore were pitiful to watch with only a few reaching safety. Upwards of 60 men were lost, and yet so near to the shore and in witness of crowds powerless to help.

Some time later while watching a display of fireworks the idea came to him to attach a line to a rocket that could be fired from a ship to the shore. Once the communication had been made a heavier rope would be hauled out and over this the crew could reach safety. Many years of costly experimentation followed before Trengrouse evolved the rocket apparatus, basically as it is today. He had hoped that every ship would

carry the equipment because most wrecks occurred with wind astern, it would be easier to fire the rocket with wind assistance. For many other reasons the apparatus was kept on shore.

Though debated in Parliament time passed with Henry Trengrouse's dying words to his son in 1854 being, "If you live to be as old as I am, you will find my rocket apparatus all along our shores." Trengrouse died a poor man despite the success of his invention with its universal application.

TREVITHICK, RICHARD

The greatest Cornish inventor, and certainly one of the greatest in world terms. Yet his fame is not so widespread as some of his lesser contemporaries.

Richard Trevithick was born in 1771 in the parish of Illogan. His birthplace formed a centre around which clustered, within a radius of one mile, the famous mines of Dolcoath, Cook's Kitchen, Pool, Tincroft and Roskear. His father was in fact manager of Dolcoath and so Richard grew up surrounded by machinery and mining processes.

He developed steam driven pumping and winding engines superior to those of James Watt by using high pressure steam, previously considered too dangerous. A few years later Trevithick turned to using steam to power a road locomotive. In 1801, on Christmas Eve, he became the first to drive a passenger

carrying engine, going up Beacon Hill in Camborne An eyewitness, Stephen Williams, reported, "Captain Dick got up steam, out in the high road, just outside the shop at the Weith. When we get see'd that Captain Dick was going to turn on steam, we jumped up as many as could, may be seven or eight of us. Twas a stiffish hill going from the Weith up to Camborne Beacon, but she went off like a little bird." The event is celebrated in the famous Cornish song:

Goin up Camborne Hill, comin down.
Goin up Camborne Hill, comin down.
The osses stood still,
The wheels went around,
Goin up Camborne Hill, comin down.

Three years later he turned to rail track setting up a ten mile length at Pen y Darren, in Wales, hauling with a steam locomotive loaded trucks of coal. This in 1804 beating George Stephenson's first locomotive by ten years!

In 1810 Trevithick went to South America to inspect pumping engines that he had installed in Peru's silver mines. After many years of adventurous travel in Central America he returned home penniless and in poor health. He died in 1833. Camborne celebrates Trevithick with a special day each year.

TRURO

Cornwall's administrative centre having both the County Hall and the County Courts. Truro became a city in 1877 when the first Bishop, Edward Benson, was installed, the cathedral being started ten years later.

The name Truro is certainly of Cornish language origin but has proved problematical to all of the place-name experts. Most agree that the first syllable must mean three.

Nothing is actually recorded of Truro before the Norman Conquest when it was one of the first towns in Cornwall to receive a municipal charter, granted by Richard de Luci between 1130 and 1140. The Municipal Guild of St Nicholas was formed about 1250 and the coinage (official stamping) of tin dates from about 1300. Truro continued to grow both in size and importance throughout the Middle Ages. Although nothing now remains Truro had a castle situated on the hill that now is the site of the County Court.

Richard Carew in his Survey of Cornwall, 1602, says of Truro, "I hold it to have got the start of wealth of any other Cornish town and come behind none in buildings, Launceston only excepted."

By 1848 Truro had become the centre of a rich and extensive mining district. It also had carpet and woollen manufacturing, an iron foundry, tanneries and potteries, together with four tin smelting works. The principal exports were tin and copper, the imports included iron, coal and timber. Truro could no longer compete with Falmouth as a port but in the late 19th century had 25 vessels registered. At Newham coasting vessels still berth while the trip boats still come right up into the city.

Architecturally, the Cathedral aside, Truro is a Georgian city. Lemon Street is a fine example, but what a pity that a cinema was allowed to devastate what was once described as the best Georgian street west of Bath. Don't miss the gem of little Walsingham Place.

Truro remains as Cornwall's major shopping and business centre with the Royal Cornwall Hospital at Treliske covering the medical needs of most. It is an area of growth, both at its centre and in the surrounding area. It is well served by schools, colleges and sporting facilities. The excellent County Museum is a must to visit.

TRURO CATHEDRAL

Designed by John Loughborough Pearson in 1880, the Cathedral was completed around 1910. Built in the Early English style, with the exception of the spires which are Norman Gothic, it is by some considered strange that such sharpness of design was chosen for a county where churches are noted for such absence. Many also believe that here was an opportunity missed, it being the first new Anglican cathedral to be built for hundreds of years, by not taking a more modern and ground breaking approach.

Built on the expanded site of the old St Mary's Church in the centre of Truro, Pearson kept the South Aisle. This giving a link between past and present with St Mary's keeping its parochial status with a unique church within a church.

The build is largely of indestructible Cornish granite together with facings of Bath stone (a soft limestone) which, unfortunately is not wearing well. The central tower is 250 feet high with a small green tower sheathed with copper.

U

UNIVERSITY FOR CORNWALL

For many years there was a demand for a university to be sited in Cornwall. For over one hundred years there was pride in the Camborne School of Mines, internationally famous and offering high level diplomas in metalliferous mining. Then, just a few years ago, the Combined Universities of Cornwall (C.U.C.) was set up. This is a partnership of six universities and colleges working together to a university degree level education.

These are:
University of Exeter
University of Plymouth
University College, Falmouth
Peninsula College of Medicine and Dentistry
Cornwall College
Truro and Penwith Colleges

In 2004 a new state of the art university college campus was opened at Tremough, near Penryn, as part of the University of Exeter (University of Exeter, Cornwall Campus) enrolling some 2,000 students. It includes the Camborne School of Mines. Just some of its graduate courses include Geography, Conservation Biology, Mining Engineering, Geology and Renewable Energy. There is a provision for postgraduate study.

The Institute of Cornish Studies is part of the University College of Humanities which supports academic research on Cornwall, both current and historical. Its first Director was Professor Charles Thomas who defined its field as, "the study of all aspects of man and his handiwork in the regional setting, past, present and future. The development of society, industry and the landscape."

W

WADEBRIDGE

A puzzling name that at first seems to contradict itself. The original crossing was a ford or 'wade'. Only after 1478 with the building of a bridge did the town grow around the bridge at the wade, hence Wadebridge. Rumour has it that to enable the bridge work to be started, bales of wool were first sunk into the soft sands to form a basic foundation. Hence the name of one of the town's inns – The Bridge on Wool. A fairly recent survey failed to find any evidence of this, but I suppose after 500 years that's not surprising! This magnificent structure, at 320 feet, the longest of its type in Cornwall, crosses the River Camel linking the town with Egloshayle (the church on the estuary) and carried a major highway. It was the vicar of Egloshayle, Thomas Lovibond, who funded its building. It has 17 arches, one of which is walled up, and was widened in 1847.

As a viable port Wadebridge needed the higher spring tides to accommodate commercial shipping. It had a short life in the 19th

century for the export of granite from the De Lank quarries, together with some china clay and iron ore.

The Southern Railway line to Padstow passed through the town. Closed in 1967 by the Beeching Act, its track bed now forms the very popular Camel Trail for walkers and cyclists.

A new bridge to carry the main road has relieved the town of its former traffic jams and has enabled Wadebridge to get on quietly with its market town existence. Apart, that is, for a few days each June when The Royal Cornwall Show (q.v.) comes to town!

WILLIAMS, JOHN & MICHAEL

The Williams family were at the heart of Cornish mining living in copper-rich Gwennap. Arriving in the County in the 17th century they became involved in all aspects of mineral extraction soon amassing a wealth that was shrewdly invested. Around 1700 the family were at Burncoose, but sometime later John Williams decided to build a new home at Scorrier, a few mile away yet still within the then greatest concentration of copper mining in the world.

John was an expert mining engineer and a very astute businessman. It was he who drove the Great County Adit, a Herculean task of some twenty years duration, which drained up to thirty mines through the outfall at Bissoe. This enabled much deeper excavations to be made with a resulting increase in ore production.

He is also remembered for having an amazingly prophetic and coincidental set of dreams. Three times in the night of 11th March 1812 he had dreams in which he saw a man about to speak to a large assembly, when another rushed forward and shot him in the back. On the following day Cornwall received the news that the Prime Minister, Spencer Perceval, had been assassinated on the same night as the dream, while crossing the lobby of the House of Commons. John Williams later visited the House and immediately recognised the setting of his dream.

A sudden upturn in the family fortune in 1845 was due to Michael Williams, third son of John, who was in London on business when he heard of a meteoric rise in the price of tin. He realised that if he could race the news home, then buy up as much tin stocks as possible, money would be made. Having caught a coach to Exeter he borrowed a horse and rode virtually non-stop to Redruth, beating the 'Quicksilver Mail' which had eight changes of horses. As planned he bought up as much tin as he could with obvious results.

WRECKING

In December 1830 three ships were aground in a gale at Portholland, between The Dodman and

Nare Head on Cornwall's South coast. Local fishermen braved the winter seas to effect a successful rescue. *The Royal Cornwall Gazette* gave a description, "Too much praise cannot be given to the fishermen of Port Holland Bay. They stripped to their drawers, not withstanding the weather was piercing cold, and after great toil and at the imminent hazard of their lives, they succeeded in getting a boat near enough to effect their object, an act of heroism worthy of British sailors."

However the local populace saw no problem with the moral dichotomy that ensued. The morning after the selfless heroism of the rescue the 'wrecking' instinct took over. Once again *The Royal Cornwall Gazette* reported, "On the following day the country people came down to the beach and in spite of the presence of three magistrates could not be deterred from their object until the crew of the revenue cutter fired at them." Their 'object' would have been to secure any or every thing of use or value that they could lay their hands on. This was the usual form of 'wrecking' as practised in Cornwall. The locals, and those from further inland, looked upon it as a right, even a God given one. Cornwall is not a county of great timber resources, nor one of affluence, therefore the very fabric of a ship together with ropes, tackle and its cargo were irresistible prizes.

There is little evidence that ships were deliberately lured onto rocks by false lights, but at times exuberance turned to violence. Legislation of 1713 hardly helped when saying that if any living creature escaped alive out of a ship then it could not be regarded as a wreck! The full Act was ordered to be read four times a year in all coastal churches and chapels. Forty years later the 'living creature' clause was omitted making it a capital offence to 'plunder, steal or take away, cargo, provisions or part of such ship.' It was also a capital offence to 'beat, wound or hinder the escape of any person trying to save his life from a wreck'.

Accounts vary on the treatment of survivors. Stories range from gallant rescue and compassion to inhumanity in the stealing of clothes from the unfortunates' backs. All in all wrecking came with poverty and the need to supplement a meagre existence. However legal it was not!

Wrecking was not peculiar to Cornwall, but we did get a name for it! A headline covering an incident at Deal, Kent was, "Wreckers out of Cornwall". In literature too the word 'wreckers' was nearly always accompanied by the adjective 'Cornish'.

So who were the wreckers? Of course those who lived near the coast, but in Cornwall the miners were a very powerful force. An observation made in 1839 was that whereas on other parts of the coast persons assembled in hundreds to plunder wrecks, in Cornwall they did so in thousands!

Considering the huge numbers involved, some indeed being shot at the scene, only a small percentage ever reached the Court. But for those that did, consider the following. In 1867, according to *The Gentleman's Magazine*, a Cornishman was sentenced to death for his part in the plunder of a wreck. The judge was clearly concerned to make an example. He admitted, in some respects, the condemned man was not so criminal as others who had escaped arrest, but as there were many common people in court he took the opportunity of "inveighing very warmly against so savage a crime, and of declaring publicly that no importunities whatsoever should induce him to reprieve the criminal." The condemned man was eighty years old. He had taken an inconsiderable quantity of cotton and a piece of rope!

WRESTLING, CORNISH

The Cornish were always celebrated for their prowess at wrestling. At the Battle of Agincourt (1415) the Cornish marched beneath a banner depicting two wrestlers in a hitch. Fuller in 1662 said, "The Cornish are masters of the art of wrestling, and to give a 'Cornish hug' is proverbial." Over 100 years ago the more important matches, some inter-county, lasted for days, while in Bodmin in 1811 the spectators num-

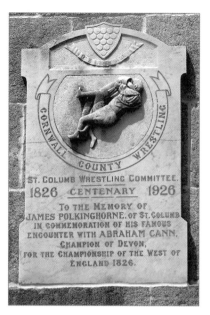

bered a thousand! After a considerable decline a revival took place when the Chapman brothers of St Wenn took to the ring. This family breathed new life into the sport.

Cornish wrestling still takes place, the contestants bare footed, wearing loose coarse jackets, and employing holds and throws. The matches are controlled by men sporting sticks, hence 'sticklers'.

WRITERS
IN CORNWALL'S PAST

To summarise the parts played in the literary scene in Cornwall is almost impossible. Many were Cornish born, with many others coming for inspiration. So expect some oversights.

Novelists that drew inspiration from th mystery and history of the county, using it as their setting, include Daphne du Maurier, Howard Spring and Winston Graham. All came to Cornwall to find a more creative environment. In Jamaica Inn and Rebecca, for instance, du Maurier writes with larger than life stories that are essentially Cornish. Spring wrote with a more realistic and less forceful style. Three years of his life were spent at Falmouth, and of the harbour he wrote, *"The sea sweeps into a magnificent harbour, and off the harbour run broad arms of water – now blue, now green – that feel their way deep into the recesses of the hills, and themselves, in many cases, throw off other arms that go in countless ramifications through the countryside."* His most famous novel was 'My Son. My Son', one of many in a Cornish setting.

Winston Graham set most of his books in Cornwall's mining history. He researched meticulously to get things right and found a new fame with the televising of the Poldark stories set in the 18th century.

One writer who came to Cornwall in 1916, staying at Zennor, was D H Lawrence. He admitted to being inspired by West Cornwall but having a German wife during wartime seemed to dull his creativity.

A contemporary of Lawrence, although with an entirely different style, who was inspired by the county, was Virginia Woolf. She was said to have gained her thoughts for 'To the Lighthouse' from looking across St Ives Bay to Godrevy.

Kenneth Graham gained inspiration for his 'The Wind in the Willows' from his frequent visits to Fowey. Readers may recognise the port's influence in the chapter 'Wayfarers All'.

R M Ballantyne, best remembered for 'Coral Island', wrote 'Deep Down', a tale of Cornish mines. He gives the name 'Wheal Dooem' to a very speculative mining undertaking.

'Q' – Quiller-Couch wrote mostly of his beloved Troy Town, the name he gave to Fowey.

The above, no doubt, had the county to thank for helping to produce good work, but two Cornish authors whose production was prolific, need to be mentioned. Silas Hocking and his brother Joseph were successful sellers of fiction, but somehow their stories don't seem to have the passion of others tending to dwell on the melancholy.

A Cornish born author, William Golding of St Columb achieved a Nobel Prize for literature. He is best known for his classic 'Lord of the Flies' written in 1954.

I do apologise for not including the many talented writers of more recent times.

Z

ZENNOR

An atmospheric village in West Cornwall lying between granite hills and the sea. It has a church, an inn – The Tinners' Arms – and a small steep-sided cove. Named from the patron saint of the church, Senara, probably from Brittany. Of interest within the church is a carved bench end depicting a mermaid.

The legend tells of a chorister called Matthew Trewella whose voice was outstanding. His singing was so clear that a mermaid in the cove heard it and was spellbound. Night after night she would listen until eventually Morvoren, as she was called in Cornish, slipped and slid her way to peer through the church doorway. When she saw Matthew singing she was transfixed letting out an involuntary sigh. The singer turned and looked at the mermaid, a dress hiding her fishy tail, and he too was besotted. With the others looking on she panicked and fled with Matthew in pursuit. With shouts of "No!" coming from his friends Matthew continued hand in hand with Morvoren until they both disappeared beneath the sea. But he was all right because on certain nights Matthew can still be heard singing beautifully above the sound of the waves.

The inhabitants of Zennor were at one time known as 'Zennor Goats'. This from the practice in

The Zennor Mermaid pew

134

the hilly areas of rearing goats to sell at Christmas for their meat.

Henry Quick was a Zennor poet who would tour the district ringing a bell and reciting his verses which usually had a religious leaning.

My father laboured underground.
Mother the spinning wheel put round.

The author D.H. Lawrence stayed here during The First World War and was captivated by the scenery. He wrote, *"At Zennor one sees infinite Atlantic, all peacock – mingled colours, and the gorse is sunshine itself. Zennor is a most beautiful place, a tiny granite village nestling under shaggy moor-hills and a big sweep of lovely sea beyond, such a lovely sea, lovelier even than the Mediterranean."* Lawrence did not find the Cornish easy to talk to. He seemed to interpret their reserved nature as a quiet form of rudeness. It may have had something to do with the fact that his wife was German. It was wartime after all! In this time of fervent nationalism some said that she was communicating with the German u-boats off shore.

The little folk museum is well worth a visit.

For Zennor Quoit see 'Quoits'.

ALSO AVAILABLE FROM PALORES PUBLICATIONS

PORTLOE
An Illustrated History
Keith Johns & Mike Rule

Keith Johns and Mike Rule have produced a wonderful feast for those interested in the history of this fascinating Cornish fishing village. From its early documentation in the Tudor and Elizabethan eras, to its current status as a well known and loved tourist venue, *Portloe : An illustrated History* covers all aspects of the village's social and economic history.

ISBN: 0-9547985-4-6

SEVEN DECADES IN VERYAN
Frank Symons

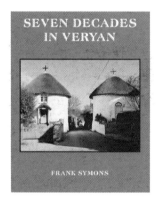

Frank Symons was born at Veryan Green in 1936. Leaving school at fifteen years of age he set-up on his own as a Market Gardener and soon had a Greengrocer's Shop. From here he sold his own produce until his retirement at the age of sixty.

Seven Decades in Veryan is a collection of Frank's recollections of the village spanning his own seventy years in Veryan.

ISBN: 978-1-906845-25-4

DRECKLY
A Collection of Possibilities

Les Merton

A collection of poetic possibilities that include . . . it could have been made to measure for any average size earth-person . . . the crush of mechanical and human traffic will surge into a terminating collision . . . a sword shining below surface, and a shot in the arm of a virtual-reality make-love-now injection.

On Planet Kernow the children are warriors . . . and the nightmare that food found in space stations comes from McDonalds or Burger King.

ISBN: 978-1-906845-24-7